The Object of

G. J. WARNOCK

Fellow of Magdalen College, Oxford

METHUEN & CO LTD

11 NEW FETTER LANE LONDON EC4

First published 1971 by
Methuen & Co Ltd
11 New Fetter Lane, London EC4
© *G. J. Warnock*
Printed in Great Britain by
Cox & Wyman Ltd, Fakenham, Norfolk.

SBN 416 13780 6 Hardback
SBN 416 29900 8 Paperback

Distributed in the USA
by Barnes & Noble Inc.

Contents

Foreword

'In offering to the public a new book upon a subject so trite as Ethics, it seems desirable to indicate clearly at the outset its plan and purpose.' That dispiriting quotation is taken from the Preface to the first edition of Henry Sidgwick's *The Methods of Ethics*; the words were written in 1874. In the century that has almost elapsed since then, books on Ethics have grown shorter, but they have assuredly not grown less frequent; so that, if the subject was trite then, one can scarcely avoid concluding that it must be much more so now. However, my own reason for thinking it desirable to indicate at the outset the plan and purpose of what follows is only in part the same as that which Sidgwick deprecatingly offered; in part it is, in a way, the opposite of his. Ethics indeed may be a well-trodden territory, but I would almost say that this book is not trite enough for comfort – that it is in some ways *strange*.

It would be a crude generalization, subject really to many exceptions but still with some discernible truth in it, to say that writings on Ethics in the tradition of English-speaking analytic philosophy have been distinguishable for many decades past into two major *genres* – those of a certain kind of general theorizing about moral judgement or moral discourse as a whole, and of comparatively restricted, detailed scrutiny of particular moral concepts or particular, limited issues. Attention to specimens of the latter sort tends inevitably to make the subject look rather disjointed; while attention to those of the former makes it look, in my opinion, empty. But that is not, or not clearly, inevitable; it is a consequence of the *kind* of general theories that have held the stage. Very early in the century G. E. Moore deployed, with what may now seem surprisingly unnerving effect, a critical weapon which he called the Naturalistic Fallacy; it was, he said, an error, an actual fallacy, to suppose that moral concepts could

be defined in terms of 'natural' concepts, or indeed that fundamental moral concepts could be defined at all. 'Good is good, and
that is the end of the matter.'[1] Now somehow – it would be a
tricky business to work out just how – this obscure but potent
doctrine of Moore's appears to have generated among analytic
philosophers a prevalent sense that the moral philosopher must
not try to say anything at all about the *grounds* of moral judgement,
about the content of moral discourse, or its actual subject-matter. It seems to have been felt that, in any such exercise, 'natural-
ism' must lurk as an error to be sedulously avoided. General
theories of ethics, then, came typically to take the form of
attempts to analyse or characterize moral concepts and moral
judgement so far only as that could be done *without mentioning* the
application of the former, or any grounds of the latter; for instance, moral terms were said to be – whatever it might be that
they were thought applicable to – 'emotive', and moral judgements to be – whatever this person or that might think were
proper grounds for them – 'prescriptive'. Of course these are
importantly distinct views; but they have in common the as-
piration to characterize moral judgement in general in a way that
will be wholly non-committal as to what it is about, and wholly
silent as to what are, or should be, or could be grounds of moral
judgement. It is in this sense that some recent general theories
seem to me to deserve – and not, no doubt, for their own part to
be at all ashamed of – the appellation 'empty'.

Now if one retains, as I do, the obstinate feeling that such con-
tent-less characterization of 'morality' is not the only possibility
– if one feels it should not be out of the question to seek to
identify and understand the subject-matter of moral discourse,
and to take up the old question (Mill's, for instance) 'concerning
the foundation of morality' – then it is difficult to evade, however much one might like to, the conclusion that the best way to
show that something of this sort could still be done is to attempt
to do it. What I feel the need for is a reasonably general 'account'
of morality, neither fragmented into unobviously related details, nor emptied of substance. To try to provide a sample, even
a rough-hewn one, of a different *genre* of Ethics seems a more
pertinent move than just to argue in general terms that there

[1] *Principia Ethica* (C.U.P., 1903), p. 6.

could be such a thing. So that is what, in this book, I have attempted to do. But the outcome is, I think, strange, and not only because the nature of the undertaking is still – though decreasingly – unorthodox. I will try to explain this.

It seems to me clear that, if one is to understand any kind or class of evaluative judgements, to see both what must and what might be appropriate or relevant grounds or standards for some species of evaluation, it is essential to try to see what that species of evaluation is done *for*, or, as one might put it, what the *interest* is in doing it. Now moral judgement is a practical matter; it is supposed to make, and often does make, a practical difference. So: what difference is it supposed to make? And how? And why is there a *need* for just that sort of difference to be made? Answers must lie in *some* features of people and of the circumstances in which people live; and if there is any merit in the Kantian idea, widely shared though of course not undisputed, that 'the moral law' is both somehow universal and basically highly stable, it seems that one is driven to look to features of people and of their circumstances that are themselves pretty universal and unapt to change. Thus one seems to be led, perhaps to one's own astonishment, to the formulation, in a style that may seem positively archaic, of vast generalizations about humans and the human predicament – to what may well look alarmingly like a kind of armchair anthropology. One is led to deal, as philosophers feel professionally uneasy in doing, in empirical assertions, and even in bald, first-order judgements of value. However, I believe this to be, though disquieting, quite unavoidable. If one seeks to present an unrefined but comparatively comprehensive, and in intention explanatory, picture of the subject-matter of moral discourse and its grounds, one cannot shy away from those very general – and fortunately, I think, not elusive or very problematic – *facts* about people and the world from which, if from anywhere, explanation must be forthcoming. The business of explanation is to make things clearer; the test of this explanation will be how far it is found to do so. A rather different ground of possible complaint is that, in presenting my picture, I have often sped silently, rapidly, and even recklessly past issues of familiar but here mostly unmooted philosophical controversy. My excuse here is that it has seemed more appropriate to my purpose to offer as plain and uncluttered a target as possible – an outline within which more detailed matters could be coherently inserted in their places, but not itself obscured by divagatory preoccupation with detail. For this reason I have not fringed my text with a mass of references to other people who have said similar things, nor taken time off, so to speak, to argue with those whose writings express or presage disagreement with me. At the same time I am, of course, conscious both of copious borrowings from others and of, in certain quarters, the certainty of dissent.

I owe several debts of gratitude. In some tentative and preliminary seminars at the University of Wisconsin in 1966, I learned a good deal, as on other occasions also, from D. W. Stampe. In collaborative classes in Oxford, and on other occasions, I have profitably discussed many of these issues with Mrs J. L. Austin. I am conspicuously indebted to Dr D. A. J. Richards of Harvard, whose supervisor I was during part of his graduate studies in Oxford, and from whom I learned a great deal more than he did from me; his own more substantial and well-armoured piece of work is, I believe, now well advanced on its progress to publication. Finally, I am much indebted to the Radcliffe Trustees, by whose munificence I enjoyed for two years more time for writing than I would ordinarily have been able to contrive; and to Mark Sainsbury who, as Radcliffe Lecturer, undertook over that period the undergraduate tuition which would otherwise have fallen to my lot.

June, 1970

1. Some Options in Ethics

It is not at all clear that what I attempt to do in this book can reasonably – that is, with any prospect of even limited success – be attempted. That being so, I had better begin by saying something very general about what it is that I attempt to do, and about some of the objections of principle – which I hope, and take, to be less than conclusive – that might well be urged against such an enterprise.

Let us begin with an objection, or at any rate a difficulty, that might be urged against moral philosophy in any form. How, it may be asked, is the subject-matter supposed to be identified? It is natural, and no doubt correct so far as it goes, to say that the concern of the moral philosopher is with the understanding and elucidation of 'moral concepts', or of 'the concepts of morality'; some would say, meaning the same thing, that his business is with 'the language of morals'. But that is by no means an unproblematic answer to the question.

In the first place, is 'morality' clearly and sharply bounded? If one considers, for instance, good and bad qualities of character, is it always quite clear which are, and which are not, *moral* qualities? When one considers that a particular act, or a particular way of behaving, is, for instance, wrong, may one not quite often be uncertain whether or not it is *morally* wrong? It is clear enough that there are good things to do that are not morally good, and bad things to do that are not morally bad but, for instance, bad policy or bad manners; but how clear is it where, or why, the line is to be drawn?

I suggest that, while there is indeed some difficulty here, it would be a mistake to become paralysed by it at this early stage. I think it is true that – except perhaps for some of those for whom morality is essentially linked to a religion – morality does, so to speak, shade off into other things, with a disputable area round it rather than a tidy frontier. But in fact this is not uncommon, and not necessarily fatal. Even subjects not commonly thought of as being afflicted in this way, like the philosphy of mathematics or the philosophy of science, are actually thus afflicted to some extent: mathematics shades off into mathematical logic, and though philosophers of science seem often, not necessarily wrongly, to simplify their problems by talking almost exclusively about physics, it is certainly not clear where 'science' stops and something else begins. (Is history a science?) What matters really is that some cases should be clear, not that all should be; physics anyway is science, even if history may or may not be, and trigonometry is mathematics, even if set-theory might be logic. Similarly, it seems not impossibly bold or naïve to make the supposition that some questions are, pretty uncontroversially, to be properly regarded as questions of morality, even if a good many neither clearly are, nor clearly are not.

Next, some philosophers, I think, regard moral philosophy pessimistically, or even with distaste, from a feeling that moral concepts are disagreeably woolly, or vague, or indeterminate; so that discussion of those concepts gives no scope for sharp-edged argument and definite conclusions, but is drearily condemned to being, in a sense, a matter of opinion – some look at these things in one way, others in other ways, and there is no hope of deciding that anyone is right or wrong. I think that this too is true to some extent, and I fully sympathize with the distaste which that thought arouses in some people. But the question, to *what* extent it is true, is itself worth considering and ought not to be prejudged; and also, if moral concepts are somehow vague or indeterminate in the way suggested, it would be a quite proper object of philosophical argument really to establish that that is so, and perhaps to try to reach some understanding of why it should be so.

In any case, the preliminary issue that I want chiefly to consider here is a different one. I want to consider the idea that the subject-matter of Ethics is, so to speak, inherently shifting and unstable because of the phenomenon of social and historical change. It is sometimes said, with obvious plausibility, that many writers on this subject have taken an excessively static, sometimes even absurdly parochial, view of their problems – assuming, as it were, that there is a fixed moral landscape, standing still to be sketched or mapped out with timeless finality; whereas in fact what confronts one is rather a Heraclitean flux, a spectacle of constant change and almost limitless diversity. Hegel, for instance, ever conscious of the march of History, has recently been commended on the ground that he was 'able to appreciate that there is no single set of concepts which constitutes *the* concepts of ethics, no language immediately available which is *the* language of morals';[1] and other philosophers have been reproved for writing as if 'there is a part of language waiting to be philosophically investigated which deserves the title "*the* language of morals"' – whereas 'in fact, of course, moral concepts change as social life changes'.[2] Perhaps the whole idea of *the* philosophy of morals is no less an unhistorical illusion than were old-fashioned notions of, say, *the* theory of the state.

There is certainly something strongly tempting in this, and no doubt something right. It is both easy and sometimes absurd to lapse into parochialism (spatial or temporal) on moral matters, and solemnly to treat as eternal verities what happen merely to be *idées reçues* of one's own community or circle, or even of one's own age-group. But I think too that the victories of an excessive relativism are often much too easily won. While acknowledging, as obviously one must, the phenomenon of change and diversity, one should also give some thought to the question: *what* changes? What exactly is it of which we must not take too static a view?

What changes, then? Well, it is uncontroversially obvious that *views* change. On questions of what is right or wrong in human conduct, good or bad, admirable or otherwise, in human character, one's own views change from time to time; the orthodoxies of one's own circle or society on these matters are apt not to be the same at one date as at another; and of course, if one brings in other societies and other ages, this diversity increases almost without assignable limit. Even a very sketchy acquaintance with history and anthropology may make one hesitate to assume that there is *any* way of behaving, considered, say, wrong

---

[1] W. H. Walsh, *Hegelian Ethics* (Macmillan, 1969), p. 79.

[2] Alasdair MacIntyre, *A Short History of Ethics* (The Macmillan Company, 1966), p. 1.

at one time and place, which has not been considered unobjectionable, or even virtuous, at another. Deliberate killing, for
instance, one might take to be an extreme case of, surely, undesirable conduct; but there have certainly been societies in
which the deliberate, unprovoked killing of strangers was regarded as not merely unobjectionable, but positively meritorious.

However, it is plainly absurd, though it is sometimes done, to
present this nearly limitless diversity as if it were a bald, brute,
irreducible fact, insusceptible of explanation, as perhaps are, for
instance, some differences of aesthetic taste. For it is really quite
obvious that these differences of view, with their consequent
differences of prevalent modes of behaviour, are at least in large
part *consequences* of other differences – of, for instance, differences
in belief about the natural consequences of actions, or, perhaps
even more importantly, the supernatural consequences. A propensity to decapitate strangers is not really surprising in one who
is convinced, however absurdly, that a regular supply of severed
heads is a necessary condition of the survival and prosperity of
his tribe; and at a less exotic level, it is clear that at least some
differences about, for instance, sexual morals are the result of
divergent beliefs about the consequences, social or psychological, of various sorts of sexual behaviour – beliefs incidentally
which, in many cases, are very far from being able to claim the
dignity of knowledge. Then it is also plainly relevant that what,
in human character and conduct, is *needed* for success, and even
for survival, varies very widely in different social and physical
conditions. Men living in, say, a prosperous commercial society
in conditions of settled peace may not greatly esteem, because
they will not encounter the need for, those traits and qualities
of character that are most highly valued by, say, horse-breeding
nomads, or jungle-dwellers, or sea-going brigands. So that
consciousness, which indeed it is desirable to have, of the huge
diversity of views that have been held as to good and bad, right
and wrong, in human character and conduct, should be tempered
by recognition that there is no reason to suppose that the *basis*
of such views is correspondingly diversified. People who hold
very different beliefs, particularly perhaps supernatural beliefs,
and who live their lives in very different conditions and in
the face of very different demands, would quite naturally arrive,

on the very same basis of appraisal, at wholly different practical conclusions.

Next, it is worth observing that, however widely forms of life, conditions of life, and views about life change, it does not actually *follow* that 'moral concepts change'. This is for the quite general reason that, as indeed is obvious, very different views may be held and formulated with the help of exactly the same concepts. It does not follow that one whose moral views are very different from mine does not employ the very same set of moral concepts that I do, or that, if I change my views, I change my concepts as well. That is to say: really to show that moral concepts change, it is not enough simply to point to the various sorts of change and diveristy which we have already, quite un-controversially, conceded do occur. For it would be entirely possible to say, in all sorts of different settings and societies, all sorts of different, even irreconcilably different things, in '*the* language of morals', if there were such a thing. Nothing that we have *yet* said establishes that there is not.

There is, however, certainly more to be said. It is a reasonable objection that the point just made is a hollow one, since, even if, as conditions, beliefs, and (consequently) views change, concepts do not *necessarily* change as well, yet they do change in fact. That may not have to be true, but surely it *is* true; as one would ex-pect. For the concepts people use are not timelessly, indepen-dently part of the furniture of the universe; they emerge and evolve, change and sometimes decay, in human thought and speech and action, and cannot but be intimately related to what people find occasion to say and do, and to what in general they think about what they say things about. One would expect communities to evolve, no doubt imperfectly and often ob-scurely, such concepts as they *need*; and this surely, communities differing so widely as they do and have done, is likely to come about in very different ways. And of course we find this to be true. Languages are not immutable; nor, particularly in the field of comment on human character and conduct, are different langu-ages always exactly inter-translatable, at any rate word for word. So surely it has to be allowed that not only do conditions, needs, beliefs, and views differ from time to time and place to place, but that concepts in fact differ as well.

Well, so they do, and of course it is as well to be aware of that. But have we said, in saying this, that moral concepts change, and consequently that there is no such thing as '*the* language of morals . . . waiting to be philosophically investigated'? Not necessarily. Of course, if 'moral concepts' are *all* those concepts which, in any society and at any time, have been employed in characterization, commendation, and condemnation, in praise or dispraise, of human character and conduct, then, since there is undoubtedly very great diversity in such concepts, 'moral concepts' must emerge as a highly diversified, historically variable set. But in fact we do not have to say this; and I want now to mention two different, indeed contrasting ways in which that conclusion can still be resisted.

What some philosophers seem to me to have held about this, often without explicitly saying so, is that (what they mean by) *the* language of morals is something of a very high degree of generality – a generality great enough to enable it, without itself changing, to accommodate a vast range of change and difference in other respects. The Naga head-hunter's way of life, his beliefs and opinions, differ widely, no doubt, from those of the Viking and the Victorian bishop; Greek diverges from English in the denomination of 'virtues'; and so on. However, in each case, it can be said, *some* people are regarded as *good* and others as *bad*; some acts as *right*, others as *wrong*; some things as what *ought* to be done, others as what ought not. Although the actual application of these very general notions has been no doubt, for all sorts of reasons, widely divergent from time to time and from place to place, the notions themselves have been standard, common property; *they* have not changed. Thus, if we take 'the language of morals' to consist essentially of such very general, non-specific terms – 'good', 'bad', 'right', 'wrong', 'ought', and perhaps a few more – we have something that there is reason to regard as floating stably in the Heraclitean flux, and to be recognized as persisting through all the diversities paraded by Hegel and the historians and anthropologists. Moral philosophy, it might be said, is concerned with the 'logic' or 'analysis' of these words and their synonyms. Though *what* is commended or condemned may vary very widely – though what are taken to be *grounds* for such judgements may be endlessly various – though specific *vocabularies* of judgement may be highly diverse and not, or not easily, inter-translatable – yet talk of good and bad, right and wrong, of 'ought' and 'ought not', in one form or another can be taken to be universal, a quite general feature of any human community at all.

But one might also, starting from just the same point, proceed in what is, in a sense, quite the opposite direction. If – one might say – on the strength of noting the various sorts of changes which, it is admitted, do occur, one concludes that 'moral concepts change', one is tacitly making an unargued, and perhaps unplausible, assumption. Namely, one is making the assumption that *all* the concepts, by means of which people have ever commented appraisingly on human character and conduct, have an equally good right to be called *moral* concepts: since those concepts admittedly change, moral concepts change. But is this reasonable? Suppose that, for instance, being struck by the vastly different character of the carvings of some primitive tribe and of contemporary sculptors, I were to conclude that 'of course, aesthetic concepts change'; it is clear that such a conclusion would be risky at best, and might be quite unwarranted. The reason for this is plain. It is that it might very well be the case that those primitive carvers were not really guided by *aesthetic* concepts at all. Perhaps their products were made for magical uses, or had some religious or ceremonial significance; perhaps they were in no sense 'artists' in the modern manner, and possibly had simply no aesthetic concepts whatever. Somewhat similarly: if, noting that A's views, even A's concepts, differ from B's at some other date, you are to conclude on that ground that moral concepts change, you have first to suppose that both A and B do have moral concepts. Otherwise, though you can of course say that concepts change, you have shown no reason for supposing that *moral* concepts do. You would not persuade me that, for instance, cricket changes, by citing some medieval game which was not cricket at all.

The suggestion here is, then, not that 'moral concepts' are so very general that one can reasonably take them to be spatially and temporally ubiquitous, but on the contrary that they are of some comparatively determinate, *special* sort, and do not change for that reason – for the reason, namely, that concepts not of that

B

sort are, not different moral concepts, but not *moral* concepts at all. It is obvious enough that this suggestion raises a question – namely, have we a way of identifying certain concepts as *moral* concepts (certain views as *moral* views, and so on) such that it is possible for us intelligibly to say of some person that, while doubtless he does have ways of appraising human character and conduct, he does not really employ *moral* concepts at all? One hesitates here before the spectre of mere arbitrariness, of uninteresting linguistic stipulation; nevertheless, it seems to me that we do have such a way, though doubtless it is not a simple matter to say what it is. The word 'moral' is intelligibly used in such a way. If we have, for instance, an individual whose views about good and bad, right and wrong, turn out to derive from a mixture of religious taboos and of passionate, exclusive devotion to the martial glory of his tribe, it seems to me that we could intelligibly say: This man does not see anything as a *moral* problem; he has no *moral* concepts at all; *morality* involves a way of looking at things which, it appears, simply never occurs to him. If he says that one of his fellow-tribesmen is a good man, because he is careful about religious taboos and has dozens of scalps hanging from his tent-pole, we could reasonably say that that is not a *moral* judgement. And it ought to be particularly observed that, in saying such things, one would not necessarily be begging any questions to the prejudice of the tribesman. For if to make moral judgements is to make judgements of some comparatively determinate sort – for instance, on some comparatively determinate basis – we do not, in saying whether or not someone makes such judgements, yet say anything at all as to whether or not he should do so. To say that the moral basis is different from that of religious taboo and tribal glory is neither to say, nor to deny, that it is *better*. That is a separate issue, to be argued separately.

In any case, I do not wish to be violently dogmatic on this matter. What I wish to insist upon is that, in moral philosophy, there are legitimately different lines to take, rather than that any one of them is *the* line that *should* be taken. My proposition, put forward in a conciliatory, latitudinarian spirit, is that there are options; let me briefly summarize those that I have distinguished.

(*a*) It is, we may agree, uncontroversially obvious that, from time to time and from place to place, there has been an immense, diversity of views as to what is good and bad, right and wrong, in human character and conduct; and it is not merely that, looking at these things in the same way, different people have arrived at different views – they have also looked at things in very different ways, taking, for instance, very different sorts of considerations to be *relevant* to the appraisal of character and conduct. So, clearly, *one* thing that one could reasonably do would be to survey this very great diversity, in the spirit of the historian or anthropologist, and perhaps try to understand it – to see how far, to take just one possibility, differing appraisals of character and conduct may derive from differing circumstances and demands of social life. One might even, perhaps running some risk of parochialism here, consider differing views and sets of views in a critical spirit, as being for instance, each in its own conditions or 'background', more or less reasonable, or intelligent, or beneficent in effect. Now if one uses, as no doubt one defensibly may, the term 'moral ideas' so widely as to cover any ideas at all, of whatever sort they may be, on the appraisal of human character and conduct, then naturally one will find that representative specimens of *every* society have moral ideas, and also that ('of course') moral ideas change as social life changes; and one will be able to regard one's undertaking as a sort of critical study of the morphology of moral ideas, or even of 'morality' in one use of the term.

(*b*) But there is also, differently from but quite compatibly with this, the possibility of a less concrete, more timeless, relatively un-historical inquiry. One may say: there is something common to all these, admittedly in many ways diverse, phenomena which (say) the anthropologist records for us; namely, they are all instances of *appraisal*, or *evaluation*, and indeed of *practical* appraisal, since we are dealing essentially with judgement of human conduct. So it is possible to consider what might be called the 'logic' of that – the general theory, so to speak, of practical appraisal, and the nature of and relations between those very general concepts which must be employed in any instance of it. If *these* are 'moral concepts', then we may well have reason to say that they do *not* change. What is done with them may change – that is, very different sorts of things may from time to

time be regarded as 'good' or 'right', and for very different reasons – but in practical appraisal *itself* we have a constant phenomenon, which can be conceptually anatomized in relatively
timeless style.

(*c*) Timelessly again, or relatively so, one may say: 'morality'
can intelligibly, perhaps usefully, be regarded as a *particular*
way, or ways, of looking at issues of character and conduct; these
things can be looked at from what is called 'the moral point of
view' – which is not just *any* point of view the adoption of which
issues in practical judgements, but a particular point of view that
can be positively identified and described. If so, it is at any rate
not obvious that *this* changes. What anthropological evidence,
for instance, gives one reason to say, is not this, but rather that,
in some societies at some dates, 'morality' perhaps is not found
at all, or is present only partially, or in some primitive state, or
something like that. If appraising character and conduct *morally*
is, not just appraising them in any practical way, but in some
particular way, one might conclude that this does not so much
itself change as gradually emerge (and perhaps sometimes dis-
appear again) *in the course* of change. And clearly, taking this
line, the central issue is going to be that of trying to characterize, and thereafter critically to consider in various respects,
what this particular mode of appraisal actually consists in.

Each of these options, it seems to me, is entirely open, and
marks out a perfectly reasonable line of inquiry. It is not that one
line or another can be said, on any *a priori* ground, to be the right
one to follow and the others wrong; they are simply different,
and each may yield interesting results in its own way. But it is,
on the whole, the third line that I shall try to follow in this book.
I propose to take it, that is, that 'morality', 'moral' judgement,
'moral' problems, and so on bring in a *particular kind* of appraisal,
or 'evaluation', of people and their possible or actual doings; and
my object is to seek some clearer understanding of this in particular. This sort of undertaking, which I think philosophers
have often embarked upon, at any rate in the past, with rather
naïve over-confidence, may by contrast be regarded nowadays
by some with considerable scepticism. I have mentioned one
major ground for scepticism already; allowing, it might be

said, that 'the moral point of view' is not just *any* point of view from which character and conduct may be appraised somehow or other, can one nevertheless reasonably suppose that it involves appraisal of, as I put it, a *particular kind* – having, that is, a fairly high degree of determinateness, and making possible the production of *a* fairly definite account? There may be something that the notion of 'morality' pretty definitely excludes; but can it be supposed that there is something *in particular* which it covers? Surely the notion is notoriously woollier, more disputable, more tolerant of diversity, than that. Well, the point is one that I do not particularly wish to argue about, at any rate at this stage. It may well be that all that a moral philosopher can do, along the sort of line that I envisage, is to offer, more or less persuasively, *a* way of looking at the subject-matter, *an* account of it, to which perfectly tenable alternatives might always be envisaged. If so, in a sense his arguments will clearly be non-cogent; but they will not necessarily, for that reason, be completely unhelpful or uninteresting. In any case, whether anything comes of this sort of inquiry can more usefully be considered after, than before, an attempt to see what comes of it. If we are, in a phrase of Berkeley's, to 'sit down in a forlorn scepticism' on this subject, at least before doing so we should put up a bit of a struggle.

2. The Human Predicament

Moral concepts come into a certain kind, or perhaps one should say certain kinds, of evaluation. By this I do not mean to say that there is any one thing which we use them in doing, but only that 'evaluation' is a good enough name for what, in one way or another, they have in general to do with. Moral discourse, in which moral concepts are employed, has to do, in one way or another, with issues about what is good or bad, right or wrong, to be commended or condemned. Obviously there is evaluation that is not moral. Good weather is not morally good; the wrong way to sew on a button is not morally wrong; commendation of your style as a golfer, or of you for your style as a golfer, would not be moral commendation. What morality has to do with is a *kind* of evaluation. The question, *what* kind, is, I suppose, just the question to which most of this book is intended to suggest an answer. Let us begin with a simpler question: evaluation of what?

There is perhaps no very useful short answer to this question; but if we had to give one, the best answer, though it immediately calls for some qualification, seems to be: the actions of rational beings. Why 'actions'? Well, it is clearly not *only* actions that are ever the topic of moral thought, or moral discussion or remark. Failures to act perhaps scarcely need separate mention. But also, people may be said to be morally good or bad; so may their characters, or their motives, or their feelings; so may practices and institutions; perhaps even objects sometimes, like books or pictures. But it seems reasonable to say that, even in these other cases, some more or less direct reference to actions is always present, and is fundamental. A person is morally good or bad primarily at least because of what he does or omits to do. A morally bad character is a disposition to act morally badly, or wrongly. Motives typically, and feelings often, tend to issue in actions. A morally objectionable institution, like slavery perhaps or an oppressive system of law or government, is morally objectionable in that it permits, or even requires, things to be done that morally ought not to be done, or prevents things being done that should be done. If a book could sensibly be said to be morally bad, that might be because writing or publishing it was taken to be a morally bad thing to do, or perhaps because reading it was thought liable to prompt people towards acting in morally exceptionable ways. So it seems that, when moral issues come up, there is always involved, more or less directly, some question of the doings or non-doings of rational beings.

Why 'rational beings'? Why not simply say 'people', or 'human beings'? The distinction is perhaps not a very important one, in practice at any rate; but still, it does seem to be the case that what makes 'people' eligible for consideration, and sometimes for judgement, as moral agents is that they are in a certain sense rational, and not that they constitute a particular biological species, that of humans. For one's doings to be a proper or possible object of moral evaluation whether by others or by oneself, it is a necessary condition that one should have at least some ability to perceive and consider alternative courses of action, to appreciate what is to be said for or against the alternatives, to make a choice or decision, and to act accordingly. But it is, one would think, a purely contingent matter that the only beings we know to exist who clearly satisfy this condition, or at any rate the only ones we commonly come across, are human beings, biped mammalian inhabitants of our particular planet. If there had been other sorts of animals on this planet, or if there were other beings elsewhere, who were rational in this somewhat minimal but essential sense, then they would have been, or would be, potential moral agents, notwithstanding the fact that they happened not to be human. One might even be inclined to regret that we come across no such beings. Our capacity to envisage a diversity of forms of life would surely be expanded by acquaintance with beings, able much as we are to choose within limits how to live their lives, but not constrained in doing so by specifically human needs, aims, and aspirations; it would be instructive to see, among other things, what morality would come down to in detail for them, and how relations between the species might be worked out (though of course they would be quite likely to work out very badly). It might have been good for humans to have had to take some non-humans more seriously than, as things are, they have occasion to do.

To be rational in this sense, then, rather than simply to be human, is a necessary condition for one's doings or non-doings to be a proper object of moral evaluation. Is it also a sufficient condition? Again the point is perhaps not very important; but for what it is worth, it seems reasonable to hold that it is not – at least in this sense, that it seems conceivable that, notwithstanding the rationality of some species of agents, questions of moral evaluation might not have arisen for them. For instance, there is the possibility, envisaged by Kant,[1] of rational beings who would not only always see straight off what action it was that in fact was morally right, or required, but would always be thereby led to do it, and would never have the least inclination towards doing anything else. For them, at least moral exhortation and persuasion would be simply unnecessary; *ex hypothesi* there would be nothing in their doings to be condemned, and perhaps, if it was simply natural to them to act in that way, moral commendation also would be out of place. A great deal, at least, that is familiar to us in moral thought and discourse would not come up in their case; for there would be no occasion for it. It is perhaps also conceivable that the circumstances of life of some species of rational beings might have been such that no moral issues ever arose for them. If, for instance, though rational, they were all completely impassive, completely invulnerable, completely self-sufficient, not significantly affected in any way by anything that went on around them, and having to do with no sentient beings of any other sort, then it is perhaps hard to see how any of their doings could be judged morally better or worse than any alternatives. It would seem to make no difference of any morally assessable sort. However, it is surely of no great importance to decide this question; for we know well enough that human beings, who are in fact the only sort of rational beings we commonly encounter, are not like this, either by nature or with respect to their circumstances. So we may

[1] *Grundlegung,* Second Section.

leave these rather fanciful speculations on one side, and move on to what we all actually know something about, that is, what may conveniently, if portentously, be called the 'human predicament'.

I had better make clear at once why I want to bring in, and indeed to start from, this perhaps archaic-looking topic. My idea is this. In general we evaluate things, it is to be supposed, for certain purposes; whenever, in any field, we rank or grade, commend or condemn, and so forth, we have – or should have, if there is to be any sense in what we are doing – some object in view, and quite possibly more than one. It is in fact risky to generalize about this, because particular cases differ so much among themselves. It might be objected, for instance, that while there will presumably be some pretty obvious 'object' in the evaluation of things that we use – for instance, to mark out the degree to which those things are good for what we propose to use them *for* – it is much less clear that we have any particular 'object' in evaluating, say, weather, or works of art. Still, at least evaluation is surely never just pointless; at the very least, even if we may sometimes have no practical purpose in view, it will be because we have some *preference* as between one thing and another that we bother at all to evaluate items of that kind. Further, it seems to me that to understand some species of evaluation (as contrasted perhaps with mastering it as a mere drill) is essentially a matter of grasping what its object is, what it is done *for*; and indeed if – *only* if – one understands this, can one be in any position to assess the appropriateness, or even relevance, of the standards and criteria employed.

Consider, for instance, the 'grading' of candidates in a school-leaving examination. Clearly, in considering how this is or should be done, it is essential to be clear as to what it is being done for. Is it the object, for instance, to determine and indicate how well candidates are judged to *have* done certain work at school? Or is it, differently, to indicate how well they are judged *likely* to do certain things in future, for instance in employment or at universities? Conceivably one might hold that these come to the same, on the ground that what a candidate has done is the only sound, or only assessable, indicator of what he may be expected to do; but if that is not so, clearly the two objects would make appropriate and relevant the employment of different criteria. Then again, it might be the object, or part of the object, to reward or reprove, encourage or stimulate, the examinees themselves; and this too would make 'grading' a different sort of exercise.

Now it is not impossible to raise the question: what is *moral* evaluation for? What is its point? Why do we distinguish between, say, actions as morally right or wrong, between people or qualities of character as good or bad? Why do we teach children to do this, by precept or example? Why do we think it worth doing? What are we trying to achieve, or bring about, by doing it? Well, it is by and large – with qualifications already noted – evaluation *of* the actions of rational beings. It does not seem plausible that in doing this we are simply, so to speak, disinterestedly awarding marks, for no particular reason or purpose, to ourselves or others. There is, it seems obvious here, some general practical end in view; and if so, it may seem manifest that the general object must be to bring it about, in some way or other, that rational beings act, in some respects or other, *better* than they would otherwise be liable to do. Put more pompously, the general object of moral evaluation must be to contribute in some respects, by way of the actions of rational beings, to the amelioration of the human predicament – that is, of the conditions in which *these* rational beings, humans, actually find themselves. Accordingly, I take it to be necessary to understanding in this case to consider, first, what it is in the human predicament that calls for amelioration, and second, what might reasonably be suggested (to put it guardedly) as the specific contribution of 'morality' to such amelioration. How are things liable to go wrong? And how exactly – or, perhaps, plausibly – can morality be understood as a contribution to their going better? These are the questions that I think worth asking. In thus talking, in archaic style, about the 'human predicament', I believe, and in a sense hope, that I shall have nothing to say the truth of which will not be immediately obvious to everyone. There are some things nevertheless that it seems relevant to say; and in a sense it would not even matter if they were not true. For the present question is really what 'morality' can be seen as pre-supposing; and the answer to that is presumably independent of the question whether all that is pre-supposed is true.

It seems reasonable, and in the present context is highly relevant, to say, without necessarily going quite so far as Hobbes did,[1] that the human predicament is inherently such that things are liable to go badly. This seems to be inherently so, but not completely hopelessly so; that is, there are circumstances, not in the least likely to change significantly or to be changed by our own efforts, which cannot but tend to make things go badly, but also something at least can be done, many different things in fact, to make them go at least somewhat better than they would do, if no such things were done at all.

In the first place, a human being as a certain kind of animal has what may be called biological needs. The life-span of humans is in any case limited; but if a person is to survive at all he must have air and water, usually shelter, and appropriate food, and he must not be subjected to gross physical damage. Apart from this there are countless other things which, while not absolute needs for every member of the species, can reasonably be regarded as indispensable enough, and indispensable for enough humans, to be called needs also. Then, in addition to and overlapping with the things that people need, there are the things that they want. (A man may not want something that he needs, if he does not know that he needs it, or even if he does know; and of course many things that we want are not things that we need.) Although there may be some things that almost every human being wants (but does not absolutely need), there is obviously also almost endless personal diversity in wants, attributable to differences of circumstances, information, and individual character and aims, or to pure vagaries of taste and fancy. Furthermore, while it seems to be a necessary truth that, if one needs something, one is at least *prima facie* and in that respect better off if one has it than if one does not, it is clear that people may want things which it would not be for their good to have, or indeed in any sense good that they should have; and sometimes they may know quite

[1] *Leviathan*, I, c. 13.

clearly that that is so. If we take a person's 'interests' to comprise those things which it is or would be actually for his good that he should have, it is evident that not only may he not know what his interests are, but he may not want to satisfy or pursue them even if he does know; and he may want to do or have things that it would not, and sometimes to his own knowledge would not, be in his interest to do or have. Attempts have sometimes been made to deny that a man may be a poor judge of his own interests, but surely wrongly. The motive, I think, has been apprehension of the practical consequences of allowing that a man might be a better judge of another's interests than that other person is of his own. It has been felt, understandably, that this, if admitted, might be taken as a pretext for a kind of paternalistic interference which, even if wholly well-intentioned, might be undesirable. But this, though understandable, is confused. If we wish to argue against the idea that a man may, quite in general, be properly compelled to act in a way which someone else thinks, but he does not, to be in his interest, we need not do so by trying to maintain that no one *could* be a better judge of his interests than he is himself. It is quite possible to maintain that, even if I do assess your interests better than you do, I am not necessarily entitled thereby to make you follow my judgement rather than your own.

Now some human needs, wants, and interests are, special and exceptional circumstances apart, just naturally satisfied by the human environment and situation, and others frustrated. For instance, there is naturally available in the atmosphere of the planet, without any intervention of ours, enough air for everybody to breathe (not always clean air, but that is another matter); and there are doubtless some things that people want to do, or perhaps would like to do, or wish that they could do, which are simply physically impossible – either completely so, for everybody, or impossible in certain conditions, or for certain people. But, uncontroversially, over an enormous range of needs, wants, and interests, these are neither just naturally satisfied, nor naturally, ineluctably frustrated. In an enormous range of cases, something both needs to be done, and also at least in principle could be done. And of course this is where practical problems arise.

Clearly, within the general area of theoretical possibility, what anyone can do, or could arrange that others should do, is limited by the availability of information, and also, no doubt one should add, of intelligence. Both in large matters of, for instance, national policy, and in small matters of purely private and personal concern, what can actually be done (except by accident) is not what could in technical theory be done, but only what is known, effectively realized, to be possible. At least as serious is the fact that the resources needed for doing things, again both in large matters and small, are practically always limited; not everything that is needed, or wanted, or would be advantageous can be done at the same time, or even could ever be done at all. This means, of course, that some 'satisfactions' must be postponed to others, with consequent problems about priorities; and some, no doubt, cannot possibly be secured at all.

This is the case, as one may put it, of attainable satisfactions competing for priority; but notoriously there are even less tractable forms of competition than this. In the first place, there is absolutely no reason to assume that the needs, wants, and interests of any one individual will just naturally form what might be called a consistent set, or coherent programme. We have noted already that a man may not want what he needs, often does not need what he wants, and may not want to get what it is in his interest that he should have; but of course it is also true that he may want things, not all of which it is practically, or even logically, possible that he should ever have. If so, there will be absolutely no reason to believe that his *total* satisfaction, meaning thereby satisfaction of *all* his needs, wants, and interests, is, in any order of priority, even logically possible, let alone practically. Then secondly, and even more notoriously, in practice people cannot but be often in competition with other people; practically at any rate, even if not in Utopian theory, it is often the case that the full or even partial satisfaction of one, or some, is attainable only at the expense of others – that is, by bringing about a situation which in some degree frustrates or does not wholly satisfy them. Nor, it seems, is this simply a practical difficulty of limited resources; for just as the wants, etc., of a single individual do not necessarily form a set such that satisfaction of all of them is possible even logically, the same may be true of the wants, etc., of pairs or of any larger groups of people. If, for instance, you want to exert absolute domination over me, and I over you, it is not logically possible that both these wants should be fully satisfied; and similarly if, say, you want exclusive possession of some particular thing that I possess, and want too.

What emerges so far, then, from even the sketchiest survey of the human predicament is perhaps depressing enough. Though perhaps not many of the things people need, or want, or would be the better for having are just naturally, ineluctably, and absolutely unobtainable (I do not say that *none* are), it is also true that not many such things are just naturally available anyway, without anything in particular being done. Human knowledge and intelligence set limits of one sort to what *can* be done; and limits of another sort are set by limited resources. Given these limitations, there is no practical possibility of everyone's having everything that he wants, or would be the better for having, or even perhaps everything that he needs. But further, there is not merely a practical difficulty here, however insuperable; for, whether for an individual or for a group (or, for that matter, for groups of groups), there is no reason to believe that total satisfaction is even a logical possibility. People may have, both as individuals and as members of groups, wants and even interests the joint satisfaction of which is not logically possible.

But of course that is not all that may reasonably depress us. Even if what we have vaguely called total satisfaction is not a practical or even a logical possibility, there is reason to think that there is a practical possibility of a good deal of satisfaction – practical, that is, from the point of view of available resources and known technical feasibility. We have been assured by a variety of prophets, in the H. G. Wells or (in some moods) Bertrand Russell manner, that, notwithstanding the perplexing diversity of people's interests and wants, and the doubtless lesser variety of their actual needs, there exist both the resources and the technical capacity to go at least a very considerable way towards the general satisfaction of the inhabitants of our planet, and not only in grossly material respects; and, discounting a little the blue-skies fervour characteristic of such prophets, there is no reason wholly to disbelieve what they say. But of course there are snags; and these have to do with certain further facts about human beings.

We have already mentioned, as limiting factors, limited resources, limited information, limited intelligence. What we need now to bring in might be called limited rationality, and limited sympathies. In the first place it may be said – certainly with extreme vagueness, but still with pretty evident truth – that human beings in general are not just naturally disposed always to do what it would be best that they should do, even if they see, or are perfectly in a position to see, what that is. Even if they are not positively neurotic or otherwise maladjusted, people are naturally somewhat prone to be moved by short-run rather than long-run considerations, and often by the pursuit of more blatant, intense, and obtrusive satisfactions rather than of those cooler ones that on balance would really be better. While mostly 'rational' in the minimal sense mentioned above – that is, able in at least some degree to envisage practical alternatives, to deliberate, and to decide – they are not all just naturally, or indeed in any other way, rational in the more exacting sense of being regularly disposed to deliberate well and to act accordingly. And this is so, of course, even where a person has to consider no interests, wants, or needs but his own.

Next, limited sympathies. This may even be too mild a term for some of the things that I have in mind. One may say for a start, mildly, that most human beings have some natural tendency to be more concerned about the satisfaction of their own wants, etc., than those of others. A man who does not like being hungry, and who is naturally inclined to take such steps as he can to satisfy his hunger, may very well care less, even not at all, about the hunger of others, and may not care at all whether anything is done to satisfy them. Even if he does care to some extent about others, it is quite likely to be only about *some* others – family, friends, class, tribe, country, or 'race'. There is also, besides complete or comparative indifference, such a thing as active malevolence, perhaps even purely disinterested malevolence; a man will sometimes be not only unconcerned about, but actively malevolent towards, others whom he may see as somehow in competition with himself, and sometimes perhaps even towards some whose frustrations or sufferings are not even supposed to be for the

advancement of any interest of his own. There are two obvious
ways in which, consequentially, things in the human predicament
are liable to go badly. For people are not simply confronted,
whether as individuals or groups, with the problems of getting
along satisfactorily in material conditions that may, in varying
degrees, be ungenial or hostile. They are also highly vulnerable
to other people; and they often need the help of other people.
But, given 'limited sympathies', it cannot be assumed that needed
help will naturally be forthcoming; and it cannot even be assumed that active malevolence will *not* be forthcoming. And perhaps above all, there may be the impossibility of trust. Whether,
in pursuit of some end of my own, I need your help, or merely
your non-interference, I may well be unable to trust you either
to co-operate or to keep out of it, if I think that you are not only
much less concerned about my ends and interests than your own,
but possibly even actively hostile to my attainment of my ends.
If so, then it may be impossible for either of us to do, either
separately or together, things that would be advantageous to us
both, and which perhaps we both clearly see would be advantageous to us both; and it may be necessary for us individually to
do things, for instance in self-protection, the doing of which
may be exceedingly laborious, wasteful, and disagreeable. It will
be obvious that all this applies as fully to relations between groups
as between individuals; and indeed that distrust and active hostility between groups has been, in the human predicament, as
frequent and constant as between individuals, and vastly more
damaging.

So far we have not, I think, said anything seriously disputable, or
at all unfamiliar. It is obvious that human beings have, in general,
an *interest* in the course of events in which they are involved: for,
though they may indeed want some things which they would not
be at all the better for having, they do have many entirely harmless and proper and reasonable wants; and they also have interests and actual needs, satisfaction of which may be absolutely
necessary for their well-being. But the course of events is not at
all likely, without their intervention, to go in a way at all satis-

factory to them; and even with intervention, there is still so much that may go wrong. Resources are limited; knowledge, skills, information, and intelligence are limited; people are often not rational, either in the management of their own affairs or in the adjustment of their own affairs in relation to others. Then, finally, they are vulnerable to others, and dependent on others, and yet inevitably often in competition with others; and, human sympathies being limited, they may often neither get nor give help that is needed, may not manage to co-operate for common ends, and may be constantly liable to frustration or positive injury from directly hostile interference by other persons. Thus it comes about that – as Hobbes of course most memorably insisted – there is in what may be called the human predicament a certain 'natural' tendency for things to go very badly; meaning thereby not, of course, in this connection, *morally* badly, but badly merely in the sense that, given the abovementioned wholly indisputable facts about people and the circumstances in which they exist, there is the very evident possibility of very great difficulty in securing, for all or possibly even any of them, much that they want, much that it would be in their interest to have, even much that they need. And the facts that make this so are facts about the *human* predicament; there is probably no great interest in speculating about possible circumstances of other conceivable species of rational beings, but still it is worth bearing in mind that the facts we have so summarily surveyed are *contingent* facts. It is easy enough to see in general terms how very different the situation would be if the beings concerned were less vulnerable, less aggressive, less egotistical, less irrational, more intelligent, more self-sufficient, and more favoured by material circumstances.

With respect to the very general limitations we have mentioned, as making it the case that things are inherently liable to go badly for people, one might raise the question whether they can be ranked in any order of relative importance. It seems to me that they can be, though probably not quite uncontroversially.

Their relative prominence, of course, will vary to some extent from case to case. Sometimes poverty of resources will be most immediately conspicuous. If things go rather badly for the inhabitants of ice-fields, or deserts, or tropical jungles, it may be

a

unnecessary to look any further for at any rate most of the explanation than to the extreme ungeniality of those physical environments. Sometimes lack of skills and knowledge will catch the eye, as in the case of people placed in intrinsically quite favourable circumstances which they lack the technical ability to make much use of. But in general it seems to me to be true, in two different ways, that more significant limits are set by other factors. It is only, after all, in comparatively unusual cases that the means of reasonable human existence are just ineluctably, physically unavailable (though it should not be forgotten that this may not always be the case); nor, one may well think (though possibly future generations will think differently), are many of the major ills of the human predicament more than partially attributable to sheer lack of knowledge and technical skills. One may well think that by far the most important matter is the poor use, or positive misuse, of resources and skills that for the most part are quite readily available; and it seems that this must be laid, in one way or another, at the door of limited rationality and limited sympathies. And in a sense these *must* always be the most important factors. For they determine what, of the things that *can* be done, *are* done; resources and skills constitute power, but power to do damage as well as to do good. Whether resources and skills are ample or very limited, it must in any case be a crucial question whether or not the use that is made of them is reasonable and humane.

But now, if limited rationality and limited sympathies are crucial, which is one to regard as the more important of the two? Perhaps it is not very sensible to attempt a definite answer to this question, if only because in practice these two factors are extraordinarily difficult to disentangle from one another. One might be inclined, pursuing much the same train of thought as in the last paragraph, to see limited sympathies as fundamental; for a man may be wholly rational, clear-headed, sane, and still, if he is not to act destructively towards others, it is essential that he should not simply see, but care, what becomes of them. Or again, if one society or group is not to oppress another, it is surely fundamental that it should not be either hostile or indifferent to that other's interests. Thus one may feel some sympathy with the common run of uplifting – if unpractical – discourses about the fundamental necessity for improvement of a 'change of heart'. But one may also feel, rightly, for two reasons, that such discourses over-simplify. In the first place, much that is most damagingly done seems really attributable, not to the malevolence of men, but to sheer folly and confusion of mind; some wars, for example, though not indeed all wars, may well seem not so much wicked as nearly insane, owing far more to short-sightedness, thoughtlessness, and muddle than to actual ill-will. So one may sometimes feel that there is plenty of good-will about, plenty of humane intentions, if only men were saner in seeing how to bring them to bear. But secondly, is it not the case that much failure of human sympathy is itself the direct offspring of un-reason? Racial hostility, for instance, is not merely – though of course it is – a gross defect of human sympathy; it is also – in common no doubt with many other hatreds, hostilities, and fears – a gross deformation of rationality. If people were saner, their sympathies also would be less stunted and deformed; hearts would be in much better shape if heads were less tangled, and haunted, and befogged. Surely it has been a very common failing of moralists, professionally pre-occupied with the weakness of good-will in human affairs, enormously to under-rate the strength in that connection, not simply of ill-will, but of sheer un-reason. It is possible conceptually to distinguish one from the other, and in practice sometimes to recognize one in the other's absence. But so often they go together, each playing into the other's hand, and perhaps not realistically to be ranked in any order of precedence.

Precedence, though, in what respect? It may well be the case that, as things are, rationality may be in shorter world supply than human sympathy, so that what we need more of at the moment is rationality. Nevertheless, there still seems to be a good case for the contention that something like (not, I hasten to say, exactly like) Kant's 'goodwill' is more fundamental still. If, for instance, I believe that you are both ready and able at any time to sacrifice me and my interests to the pursuit of your own, I shall not be reassured by any decrease in your muddle-headedness – unless, indeed, as might very well not be the case, in an un-muddled perspective the sacrifice of me would be seen to be irrational from your point of view. Rationality in fact seems, like intelligence and skill and resources, to be something that can be used to do harm (at least to some) as well as good; what is ultimately crucial is *how* it is to be used. Nothing in the end, then, seems to be more important, in the inherent liability to badness of the human predicament, than that limitation which I have called, vaguely enough, 'limited sympathies'.[1]

Now, the general suggestion that (guardedly) I wish to put up for consideration is this: that the 'general object' of morality, appreciation of which may enable us to *understand* the basis of moral evaluation, is to contribute to betterment – or non-deterioration – of the human predicament, primarily and essentially by seeking to countervail 'limited sympathies' and their potentially most damaging effects. It is the proper business of morality, and the general object of moral evaluation, not of course to add to our available resources, nor – directly anyway – to our knowledge of how to make advantageous use of them, nor – again, not directly – to make us more rational in the judicious pursuit of our interests and ends; its proper business is to expand our sympathies, or, better, to reduce the liability to damage inherent in their natural tendency to be narrowly restricted. We may note at once that, if this is, as I think, in a sense the most important of the built-in tendencies of things to go wrong, the present suggestion fits well with the common idea that there is something peculiarly *important* about morality. But that is too vague to be much use. The only way, I suppose, to see whether there is anything much in this suggestion – to see whether it illuminates the nature of 'the moral point of view' – is to see what follows from this general supposition, how it works out, and whether what it would imply is closely consonant enough with what we already think we know about moral judgement. It must be remembered, of course, that quite different ways of looking at the matter might quite well issue in just the same implications, so that argument of this pattern is certainly not demonstrative. But we may give it a try, and see how persuasive we can make it look.

[1] Some more extended remarks on this topic, though not, I fear, much clearer ones, are offered in Chapter 9, below.

3. Utility

In this chapter, which will be a brief one, I want to consider what is, I suppose, the simplest of all suggestions as to how exactly 'morality' is to be envisaged as contributing to betterment of the human predicament – a suggestion tempting, no doubt, in its apparent simplicity, but nevertheless to be rejected, I think, on a number of not unfamiliar grounds.

The suggestion to be considered here arises naturally enough out of reflections of the sort outlined in the previous chapter. As was there suggested, if one considers the pretty uncontroversial liability of things to go badly for people, given the general character of the human predicament, one may reasonably come to think that a specially important constituent in that liability is what we there called the limitedness of human sympathies – the propensity, natural to some degree in all human beings, not to care about, to be indifferent or even actively hostile to, the welfare, needs, wants, interests of other humans, and conversely to be concerned about, if not exclusively their own, yet those of some more or less restricted group. Now, if that is reasonable, and if it is reasonable also to suppose that it is essentially at this point that 'morality' is supposed to do some good or countervail some harm, the simple idea may well occur to one that this countervailing influence can be supposed to operate, so to speak, directly and head-on. The essential evil to be remedied, on this view, is the propensity of people to be concerned in practice, if not exclusively with their own, yet with some restricted range of, interests and ends; and surely the *direct* way to counter, or to limit, the evils liable to result from this propensity is to counter it *itself* – to inculcate, that is, a directly remedial propensity to be concerned with, and in practice to take into account, the welfare, needs, wants, interests of *all*. This is, I think, at least one way of regarding the thesis of simple Utilitarianism. If we say (riding, no doubt, rather rough-shod over complexities of exact formulation) that things are liable to go importantly wrong because of one's natural tendency to be practically concerned with the 'happiness' exclusively of oneself or of some, we may find it persuasive to go on to suppose that morality proposes the directly countervailing, single end of the 'general happiness', or 'greatest happiness of the greatest number'. On this simple view, then, there would really be only one basic moral virtue, that of universal beneficence, though no doubt more specific terms might be introduced to name the various exemplifications of this one virtue in various special cases. And on this view moral evaluation, though no doubt often difficult in practice, would always be very simple in theory. A person would be morally good or bad, exactly in proportion as he displayed in his conduct this single virtue of universal beneficence; his acts would be morally right or wrong, exactly in proportion as each furthered the single general end, or failed to do so; and so on.

One ground on which this simple but not utterly unplausible view has often been attacked is that it would make the task of moral evaluation, however simple in theory, in fact intolerably vague and indeterminate, or even impossible. How, it is rhetorically demanded, is 'happiness' to be assessed? How can I be sure in exactly what degree, or even whether in any degree, the 'happiness' of others, or even of myself, would be affected by each of what may be very many different courses of action open to me? I may know pretty well what I want, or some other person wants, here and now; but future wants are relevant too, and what about those? Can I possibly assess the effects that my action may have on the happiness of *everyone*? Can I even know, with any tolerable degree of assurance, what the effects of any action of mine, stretching out into a limitless future, will actually be? How are different happinesses, so to speak, to be compared and computed? Is it better to make, say, twelve people moderately happy, or six people very happy indeed? Perhaps the latters' increment of happiness would be 'twice' that of the formers' – but does that really make sense? Is ten very happy, and one very miserable, better or worse than eleven moderately happy? One happy for half an hour, than two for a quarter of an hour? And, in any case (some would add) what is so uniquely important about *happiness*? Is it better to be happily sozzled than un-cheerfully sober? *Morally* better?

It is easy to be swept away by torrents of argument of this sort; and certainly it has often been supposed that simple Utilitarianism can be briskly and conclusively swept away in just this fashion. But points of this sort are not really, I think, all that impressive. In the first place, if the conclusion of argument of this sort is that, on this view, the task of moral judgement will be extraordinarily difficult, one may ask whether there is any good reason for supposing that it is actually simple. And of course there is not. Moral problems are often extremely difficult to resolve; I know of no reason to suppose that they are always soluble at all. So one might even be inclined to reverse the argument at this point, and say that any account of morality must be mistaken which does *not* yield the consequence that moral judgement is sometimes, and may be often, exceedingly difficult. In any case, were not the difficulties considerably exaggerated? I do not, on this doctrine, really have to think about *everyone*, except in the highly unlikely circumstance that absolutely everyone would be significantly affected by some action of mine; those actually involved will often be not numerous at all. Nor need I, usually, pursue my deliberations into the ramifying and fog-bound delta of a limitless future; for the effects of my action, seriously attributable to me, seriously to be seen *as* effects of my action, may be reasonably certain and not very remote. And as to the difficulty in comparison and computation of 'happinesses', it is at any rate clear that such comparisons do somehow get made; I decide that Aunt Jane will be happier, living with Cousin Joan, than she would be in a nursing-home, and that, though this arrangement may possibly detract from the happiness of Joan, the plus, so to speak, on Jane's side of the balance outweighs the minus quantity accruable to Joan. We also take duration and number somehow into account; although my pile-driving operations will considerably distress, say, fifty people, which is a more serious matter than just one or two, there counts the other way the fact that it will not be for long. In fact, when one comes to think of it, it is really absurd to suppose that simple Utilitarianism could be wholly brushed aside on such grounds as these alone. For its thesis reduces, we suggested, to the contention that beneficence is really the sole and sufficient moral virtue; now, that may not be true; but beneficence surely is *a* moral virtue, and not a merely theoretical one which it is actually impossible in practice ever to exercise. To reject the thesis on these grounds alone would amount to maintaining that beneficence itself, the general disposition to 'do good', to spread sweetness and light, is so much clogged by imponderables, incalculables, and unpredictability as not to be a practical proposition at all. But that is surely not true. It may not be easy to be effectually beneficent, but it is not always impossible.

A more telling contention – and I think, though it needs more defence than it is sometimes given, ultimately a correct one – is that just hinted at; namely, the contention that, while generalized beneficence no doubt is a moral virtue, it is not the only one, and hence that 'doing good', in the way of promoting and cultivating 'greatest happiness', cannot be the sole criterion of moral right and wrong. There are other virtues, not reducible to specialized forms of beneficence. An action may be, for instance, just, but not more beneficent in its effects than would have been any other action possible in the circumstances; or maximally beneficent, but still to be morally condemned as unjust. It might be that, in easily imaginable circumstances, you would greatly decrease my happiness by telling me the truth; but it seems at least not immediately and undeniably to follow that it would be morally right for you to tell me a lie, or even to refuse to tell me anything at all. If I have made some fairly trivial promise to you, it is not obvious that I am morally justified in breaking it for the sake of purveying some rather greater good to a third party. And so on. The common view is, it has been held, and I think perfectly correctly, that the beneficent promotion of Utility, of happiness all round, is merely *among* the pertinent concerns of morality; this is no doubt a morally proper end, but there are bounds to its permissible pursuit set by *other* moral requirements which cannot be accounted for in terms of this end alone.

But it is not quite satisfactory, nor is it necessary, simply to say this and to leave it at that. If one says this and no more, it is open to the simple Utilitarian to change, so to speak, the banner under which he marches; if it is conceded that, in the common view, there are requirements of morality not reducible to, not explicable in terms of, the single virtue of felicific beneficence, then he cannot, of course, claim that his contention elucidates what *is* the current concept of morality, but he can contend instead that his thesis sets out what it *should* be. He may present himself – as, historically, Utilitarians have always been very ready to do – not as a mere elucidator, but as a reformer, a revisionary. Perhaps we *do* not morally approve beneficent lies, beneficent injustices, or beneficent breaches of faith; but perhaps we *should* do. It is not enough simply to say that this would be unorthodox; for of course it may be that received orthodoxies in morals, as in politics and many other spheres, are really irrational, and ought to be abandoned so far as they cannot be squared with what is offered as the really rational criterion.

So what more can be said?[1] Well, it can, I believe, be effectively argued that this proposed reform would not really be rational at all, in the comparatively precise sense that it is extremely ill calculated to contribute to the end supposedly in view – namely, betterment, or non-deterioration, of the human predicament. Paradoxical though it may at first sight seem to say so, this end is *not* most effectively to be pursued by general adoption of the sole over-riding object of pursuing it.

Why is this so? The following analogy may be of some help here. Suppose that, to confront an enemy on the field of battle, I assemble, say, fifty thousand men, all fired with the single over-riding aim of victory. What will be the best way of securing this end? It does not seem – in this case – at all paradoxical to say that the end will *not* be most effectively pursued by telling each man so to act as, in his judgement, best to achieve it; even if all my men are highly sagacious and experienced soldiers, mere chaos will ensue, since the task thus set them is not merely difficult, but completely impossible. Clearly enough, none can act effectively entirely on his own; but equally clearly, none can tell what his part should best be in any corporate enterprise unless he knows how others are going to act – and how he can know that, since each is faced with just the same hopeless uncertainty as he is himself? Even if my army should manage to

[1] In the remainder of this chapter I liberally plunder, and rather ruthlessly over-simplify, some of the subtle contentions of D. H. Hodgson's *Consequences of Utilitarianism* (O.U.P., 1967).

get itself on parade – and it is not really clear how it would manage to do even that – any ensuing action, however splendidly intentioned on the part of each, would be a mere welter of conflicting, unco-ordinated, self-defeating, unvictorious confusion.

But, it may be objected, in saying this I am not crediting my soldiers with much intelligence; for surely, in such a case, they will see that the end that each has in view is to be pursued, not by each on his own going bald-headed for that end, but by the appointment of commanders, to make plans and issue orders for their execution. But how is this actually supposed to work? It is, I suppose, orthodox military doctrine that, except perhaps in very exceptional circumstances, a military subordinate is to comply with an order that he is given, whether or not his doing so is, in his opinion, or even in fact, most conducive to the agreed end in view. But this, of course, is to say that the subordinate's criterion of action is to be obedience to orders, *not* his judgement of what is most conducive to the end of victory; and if my soldiers are really to be guided by this latter criterion alone, then their acceptance of the former one can be only conditional – each will obey the orders of his superior commander, *provided* that he thinks it most conducive to victory to do so. But here trouble lurks. For if subordinates make this reservation, then they may see reason sometimes to disobey an order. But their commander will know that, and accordingly may find it necessary to confine himself to orders such that it will not be too disastrous a matter if they are disobeyed. But this in turn his intelligent subordinates will appreciate; and thus of course it will weigh less with them that some contemplated action of theirs would be in breach of an order. The chance of their disobeying orders is thereby increased, and consequentially the non-seriousness, so to speak, of the orders they are given. And the upshot may be that their 'commander' will have no reason to think that his issuing 'orders' will make any difference at all, so that we are back in the unpromising welter of the previous paragraph. It thus appears that, if the end of each and all is to be effectively pursued, it is actually necessary in such a case that promotion of this end should *not* be each man's sole criterion of practical decision; on the contrary, each man must be prepared to do, must think it wrong not to do, some acts which, in his judgement and perhaps also in fact, are not such as to promote that general end.

This case may seem special and artificial; but the point is a quite general one. Suppose next that I, a simple Utilitarian, entrust the care of my health to a simple Utilitarian doctor. Now I know, of course, that his intentions are generally beneficent, but equally that they are not *uniquely* beneficent towards me. Thus, while he will not malevolently kill me off, I cannot be sure that he will always try to cure me of my afflictions; I can be sure only that he will do so, *unless* his assessment of the 'general happiness' leads him to do otherwise. I cannot of course condemn this attitude, since it is the same as my own; but it is more than possible that I might not much like it, and might find myself put to much anxiety and fuss in trying to detect, at successive consultations, what his intentions actually were. But conspicuously, there are two things that I could not do to diminish my anxieties: I could not get him to promise, in the style of the Hippocratic Oath, always and only to deploy his skills to my advantage; nor could I usefully ask him to disclose his intentions. The reason is essentially the same in each case. Though he might, if I asked him to, promise not to kill me off, he would of course keep this promise only if he judged it best on the whole to do so; knowing that, I could not unquestioningly rely on his keeping it; and knowing *that*, he would realize that, since I would not do so, it would matter that much less if he did not keep it. And so on, until his 'promise' becomes perfectly idle. Similarly, if I ask him what his intentions are, he will answer truthfully only if he judges it best on the whole to do so; knowing that, I will not unqualifiedly believe him; and knowing *that*, he will realize that, since I will not do so, it will matter that much less if he professes intentions that he does not actually have. And so on, until my asking and his answering become a pure waste of breath. And this is quite general; if general felicific beneficence were the only criterion, then promising and talking alike would become wholly idle pursuits. At best, as perhaps in diplomacy, what people said would become merely a part of the evidence on the basis of which one might try to decide what they really believed, or intended, or were likely to do; and it is not always obvious that there is much point in diplomacy.

Can one say that what simple Utilitarianism essentially defeats is the possibility of *co-operation*? It seems that, if two or more persons are effectively to co-operate, in wars, in professional pursuits, in business, or even in conversation, there must be such a thing as being prepared to be, and recognized as being, *bound* to specific requirements of the co-operative 'ethics', or to specific undertakings. It is not, one may thankfully observe, essential that such bonds should absolutely never, with or without excuse, be broken; but it is essential that they should not in general make absolutely no difference, count simply for nothing one way or the other. But, if general beneficence is to be our sole criterion, they would inevitably count for nothing; they would be accepted with reservations, hence not relied upon, hence more readily disregarded and less relied upon, and so on to the point of wholly vanishing significance. And thus, towards the betterment of the human predicament, the simple recipe of general beneficence must be, while admirably intentioned, very minimally efficacious. If this were everyone's sole criterion of right and wrong action, it may reasonably be supposed that comparatively little direct harm would be done, but also very remarkably little good. For how much good can we do, if we cannot even usefully communicate?

Recognition of the shortcomings, or of some of them, of what we have been calling 'simple' Utilitarianism has led to the suggestion of an amendment, familiar in the literature as 'Rule-Utilitarianism'. The suggestion here is that the strategy, so to speak, of morality is to be construed on a less direct, bald-headed plan. Instead of seeking to counter the evils of 'limited sympathies' by a simple, head-on, exclusive attachment to general beneficence, it is suggested that morality functions, *somewhat* analogously with systems of law, as a system of *rules*. Particular acts, then come out as morally right or wrong accordingly as they conform or do not conform with the rules; and it is the *rationale* of the rules, not of individual acts, that they contribute, or would contribute if generally complied with, to betterment of the human predicament. In this potentially rather complex doctrine there is, I believe, enough both of truth and error to warrant careful attention; and we had better begin by considering the notion of a rule.

4. Rules

A rule, in the sense in which rules will be considered here, is something which prescribes, proscribes, or (sometimes) licences the performance or non-performance of certain actions, or, less pompously, the doing or not doing of certain things. There will practically always be restrictions of one sort or another on those to whom a rule 'applies' – for example, to a specified (or implied) particular group, as in rules for the conduct of undergraduates, or to any persons in a particular place, as in rules about smoking in the library, or to persons engaged in a particular way, as in rules of a game; and a person can be said, I take it, to comply with or break only a rule that does actually apply to him. I do not break the rules of golf when playing cricket, or comply with them either; outside the library, I may smoke, or not, without breaking or complying with the library's rules. What *is* complying with a rule, or breaking it? Not, one may think, *just* acting or abstaining as, or not as, the rule requires; for one might do either without even knowing that the rule existed; and although one might possibly be said to break a rule unwittingly, simply in doing what in fact the rule proscribes, it sounds strange to speak of unwitting compliance with a rule – if I do not know of the rule, or perhaps do not understand it, my conduct may conform to the rule's requirements, but is not, I think, compliance. (I cannot obey an order which I do not receive, though it may happen that I do what the errant order required of me.) It seems to be a minimum condition for a reasonable rule that it *can* be complied with; for if not, the rule will be quite useless, or perhaps misplaced. It would be useless to make rules such that those for whom they were made would never know of them, or could never understand them even if they did know; and it would be misplaced to make rules about the doing or non-doing of things where those concerned had no choice as to whether to do those things or not – a rule prohibiting illness, for example, would be out of place, but not of course rules requiring due care for one's health. One might say that, if there is to be any *point* in a rule, it must be supposed that those to whom it is 'applicable' at least can know what it is, and can act as it requires; for if that is not so, it will simply make no difference whether there is a rule or not. So much is obvious.

It is worth observing, next, that there are certain questions which reference to a rule may give appropriate occasion for, and to which it is reasonable to require that there should be answers. These are, non-exhaustively no doubt: first, why have, or why is there, a rule at all? Second, why *that* rule? Third, why should one, or why should I, comply with the rule? And fourth, there may of course be the question: *is* there such a rule? Does the rule purportedly referred to really 'exist' (whatever that means)? I think we may get further light from considering these questions.

First, then, why have a rule at all? It seems clear that this question will always need an answer of some sort. For there is always an alternative to having a rule, namely, leaving things, or leaving people, to go on as they may; and since it is difficult to see how having rules could be regarded simply in itself, for its own sake, as a good thing, there needs to be a reason for *not* just leaving things alone. The general form of a reasonable answer also seems clear, and has two parts: it would need to be claimed, first, that the sort of action, or of behaviour, in which compliance with the rule in question would consist, is in some way desirable, and second, that the existence or institution of a rule increases, or would increase, the likelihood of its occurrence – in that, for example, it could not safely be supposed that people would so act anyway, even without a rule. But of course such a frame admits of very different fillings. In premises in which there is a serious risk of fire, it will clearly be desirable, for safety's sake, that people should not smoke; and unless it is already clear for some other reason, for instance that all those concerned are less than six years old, that they are not likely to, there will be a case for having a rule against smoking there. Sometimes what is desirable in compliance with a rule may, for any of a range of reasons, be simply uniformity – it may not greatly matter whether this or that is done, but only that, whichever is done, those concerned should all do the same. Sometimes the object is clarity, or the reduction of uncertainty; it may not matter much in itself whether or not a certain thing is done, but be undesirable that whether it should be done or not should be, as it might be in the absence of 'regulation', a frequent topic for argument and dispute. And sometimes, perhaps surprisingly at first sight, the object of a rule may be to make some performance more *difficult* than it would otherwise be; naturally this is not in general a desirable thing, but it often is in the particular case of games. Unless the business of getting the ball into the opponents' net was made artificially difficult by the rule that only the goal-keeper may touch the ball with his hands, soccer would not be the game of skill that it is, or at any rate not the same game. Such a rule can be distinguished from rules, for instance, against the infliction of deliberate injury, which is, most would think, undesirable in any case. Bull-fighting would be a dull business, and not merely a repulsive one, if all that the matador had to do was, somehow or other, to kill the bull.

It is sometimes said in this connection that there are 'two sorts' of rules, which it has become common to distinguish under the terms 'regulative' and 'constitutive'.[1] The suggestion is that some rules merely 'regulate' some, so to speak, pre-existing activity – they stipulate, for instance, *how* something is to be done which people would, or at least could, have done anyway, whether or not there had been a rule; whereas other rules, for instance those of a game, are said to 'create the possibility' of doing something, namely playing that game, which (logically) without those rules could not be done at all. This, however, is somewhat confused. In the first place, all rules, not merely some of them, are 'regulative' – that is, there is always *some* way of saying what a person acting as some rule requires would be doing, which makes no mention of that rule, and therefore there is always something that he could do, whether or not there were such a rule; and in the second place, while perhaps only some rules are 'constitutive' – that is, there is only sometimes a special term for compliance with or breach of a rule, into the 'sense' of which the rule essentially enters – it is clear that there always

[1] See, in particular, J. R. Searle, *Speech Acts* (C.U.P., 1969), pp. 33–42.

could be such special terms, and it is often more or less accidental whether there actually are or not. This supposed distinction between 'two sorts' of rules is really, I think, a confused groping after two other distinctions. There is, first, a distinction between two ways of saying what people do – one way which, as for instance walking, or hitting balls about, or waving flags, involves no reference to any rules, and another which, as for instance playing tennis, or signalling, or bequeathing property, does essentially make reference to rules, or presupposes them. Then, second, there is a broad and rather woolly distinction between two different 'objects' of rules, or reasons for having them. It is not the *object*, presumably, of the criminal law to 'create the possibility' of committing criminal offences, though of course it incidentally does so; the object is to 'regulate' in certain respects the conduct of members of society. By contrast, while the rules of, say, soccer do 'regulate' the way in which balls are kicked about in fields, it is in this case the *object* of (some of) the rules to 'constitute' a certain exercise in physical skill and ingenuity, to 'create' a particular game for people to play. If we do wish to distinguish different 'sorts' of rules – as we might do, no doubt, in very many very different ways – *one* way at least would be by reference to what the rules are *for*; but they have in common that, if reasonable, they must be for *something*.

One can see in outline, in any case, how there may be many and various reasons for having rules – and also, sometimes, for having no rule at all. Perhaps none is needed, since what the rule would require is, by and large, going to happen in any case. Perhaps, very differently, a rule would be ineffective, since there is reason to suppose that it would not be complied with. Perhaps it would be pointless, since compliance with it would not be preferable in any clear way to what would happen if things were simply left alone, to go on as they might. And no doubt one should mention here the further possibility that, even if compliance with a rule might be expected and would on the whole be desirable, objection might still be taken to the institution of a *rule*. What I have in mind here is the intelligible notion that, even if, say, the pupils at my school should show certain marks of respect towards their mentors, and even if, left to themselves, they are apt not to do so, it may still be undesirable that they should be required to do so by a *rule*. Some performances, one may intelligibly think, are not of much value unless they are quite freely undertaken by their performers; if so, there is a special reason here for keeping rules out of it.

Consider next the question: why *that* rule? Here we should notice, no doubt, the familiar distinction between explanation and justification – between, for example, explaining historically how some rule of Parliamentary procedure came to exist, and justifying with reasons its continued existence; our interest here is in justification. Sometimes there may, for a particular rule, not be any – to take the hackneyed case, while it makes obvious sense to have *some* rule prescribing how vehicles are to be driven on public roads, there is no particular reason for prescribing the left of the road rather than the right; this is a case where some uniform practice is desirable, rather than any one in particular of some alternative practices, so that, while a case may be made for having a rule, there is really no distinguishable case for having *that* rule. But this seems not usual. More usually, there seems to be the supposition, not just that *some* rule-following behaviour is desirable, but that a particular sort of such behaviour is desirable; and in such cases the question of justification will be, first, whether the sort of behaviour thus aimed at really is desirable, and second, whether the particular rule is really such that its 'existence' tends to promote that sort of behaviour. (On this last topic, one might sometimes wish to distinguish criticism of a rule from criticism of some *formulation* of a rule; one might sometimes wish to say that, while some rule was all very well, some particular formulation of it was clumsy, or unclear, or provocative or something of that sort.) Clearly, the sort of reason for which a particular kind of rule-following behaviour is judged to be 'desirable' will be very different in different cases. For example, rules concerning the inheritance of property may raise large issues as to what is desirable or otherwise in social policy; whereas a new rule of cricket, for instance, may call for action which is 'desirable' merely as tending to make cricket less tedious to watch.

So what about compliance? Up to a point it seems that no separate question arises here. If, for instance, impressed by the risk of fire in the library and by the likelihood that some people, left to themselves, would indulge in smoking there, I conclude that there ought to be a rule against smoking, I can scarcely regard it as a separate question why, if such a rule were in force, people should comply with it. For of course, if there were no reason why they should, there could be no reason for having the rule in the first place; the reason for having the rule, namely that smoking on these premises is undesirable, and specifically dangerous, is obviously *also* a reason why, if such a rule exists, it should be complied with. But this point cannot, I think, safely be generalized. For while it is, obviously, implied *prima facie* that any rule should be complied with by those to whom it applies – a rule could scarcely carry the general rider that 'this rule need not be complied with by anybody' – there surely are rules such that, while their 'existence' is well justified, no one would suppose that they should *always* be complied with, by everyone. For there may often be good reason to say that it does not really matter; playing non-competitive golf on a Saturday afternoon, one really need not stick to *all* the rules of golf, desirable though it doubtless may be that such rules should exist, and be complied with on more solemn and keenly competitive occasions. Thus, while, if I think that there is *never* good reason for compliance with some rule, I can really offer no reason why there should be that rule at all, I may quite well think that there should be a certain rule, but no reason why *everyone* it applies to should *always* comply with it.

But now, if I think that one should comply with some rule, either always or at least sometimes, do I necessarily think that that rule should exist? Plainly not, I think. For even if I do not think, abstracting as it were from the rule, that there is any special reason why people should behave as the rule requires of them – and hence do not think that the rule ought to exist – I may yet think that, if it does exist, it should be complied with. There are, I suppose, at least two sorts of reasons for which one might think this. First, in cases in which sanctions are attached to breaches of rules, it may to that extent be merely prudent for people to comply with them, even if the rules seem utterly pointless or even objectionable; and second, one may sometimes think, as no doubt law-abiding persons often do, that an authoritative rule-making body ought to be accorded the respect of obedience, even by those who may not, in some cases, view with approval or even understanding some particular rule which it promulgates. Rather differently, even if I were to think for some reason that it would be far better for traffic to drive on the right of the road, I will have obvious reason to think that no one should do so, so long as 'the rule of the road' prescribes the left-hand side. It is evident, however, that the mere *existence* of a rule does not by itself provide a reason why it should be complied with; it must be possible to point to *some* objection to non-compliance, other than simply that it *is* non-compliance, if we are not to regard rules themselves with a kind of idolatry. Whatever one may think of obedience as a virtue, it is scarcely to be supposed that obedience towards just anything and anybody, all other considerations apart, could be, even *prima facie*, a good thing. This holds, I think, even in those cases in which what rules are *for* is primarily to 'constitute' some rule-defined activity – though here, indeed, the only 'reason' for compliance with the rules may be that, if one does not comply with them, what one does will not count as engaging in that activity at all, or will be regarded as not engaging in it 'properly'. It is sometimes said that rules 'provide reasons for acting'; and one may agree with that, subject, however, to the general requirement that they not only exist, but are reasonable rules.

Consider next the question why some particular person should comply with some rule. No doubt the question 'Why should I?' is sometimes just a way of introducing the question 'Why should anyone?', and as such raises no separate issue. But it may raise a separate issue, in at least three ways. First, I might raise the question why I should comply with some rule, if I thought that I was or might be not one of those to whom the rule 'applies'. Undergraduates, let us say, are to wear gowns when attending lectures; but why should I? Perhaps I am not an undergraduate of this university, or not an undergraduate at all. But it is worth noticing that, even if I am quite clearly not one of those to whom some rule applies, it does not in general immediately follow that there is no reason why I should act as the rule requires; for there may be some special reason why I should. For me not to do so might be, for instance, discourteous, or inconvenient – even if the rule, strictly, does not apply to me, so that strictly I am not in a position to comply with or break it. But often no such question arises, or even could arise; I could not possibly act as is laid down by, say, the rules for the conduct of an examination, if I have nothing to do with the examination at all. One way, no doubt, in which rules may be defective is by leaving it *unclear* to whom they apply; there will be trouble with rules, say, for the conduct of 'resident members', if it is unclear what counts as being a resident member. But no doubt also, however clear one tries to be, it will be difficult or impossible absolutely to exclude the possibility of marginal or otherwise disputable cases.

Secondly, we should mention here the obvious possibility that, though some rule may be perfectly approvable in general, and I may clearly be one of those to whom the rule applies, I may think that *in this case* I need not, or even should not, comply with it – that is, that a breach of the rule is on this occasion 'justified', or even required. I have in mind here not the case already mentioned, where one may think that non-compliance with some rule sometimes does not matter, but the case – or rather, the enormous range of cases – where compliance with a rule may be thought to be out-weighed by quite other considerations. There is perhaps nothing to be said quite in general about this, except that, as of course is very obvious, the applicability in a certain situation of some rule, however 'good' the rule may be, is not in general a *conclusive* reason for acting, in that situation, as the rule requires; thus, it is always possible that one might ask, without questioning either the rule or its applicability: should I – or, why should I – comply with it here and now? The question here is, not whether there is *any* reason to act as the rule requires, but whether there may not be – as there might be – better reason, here and now, for acting otherwise.

Then thirdly, perhaps we should take note of a different sort of reason I might have for supposing that compliance by me, here and now, does not really matter. The object, so to speak, of a rule against smoking in the ammunition store is, no doubt, strictly that *no one* should smoke there; and if there is good reason for that, then there is good reason why I should not. But one might argue that the real object of a rule against, say, walking on the grass is not really that no one, but rather that not *too many* people, should do so; for the occasional transient would do the grass no harm, and the general prohibition is really a mere surrender to the difficulty of otherwise limiting transients to a harmless number. If so, why should I not, harmlessly, break that rule? Well, in such a case non-compliance can be argued against, and often effectively. Perhaps my example would undermine the desirable general practice of complying with the rule; perhaps it is not for me, or for any other individual, to be judge in his own cause as to whether or not to comply; perhaps, if I break this rule, my own character will thereby be nudged along the downward path; perhaps it is simply unfair for me not to do what other people, as I concede rightly, are required by the rule to do; or perhaps I cannot get away with it. But that such argument must always be effective seems excessively strong doctrine. If occasionally, alone and in pitch darkness and wearing plimsolls, I nip across the forbidden grass, I will surely have a very tender conscience indeed if I do so in the conviction of doing wrong.

I turn now to the tricky and, for our purposes, crucial question of what it is for a rule to 'exist', for there to be a rule. Sometimes there is surely no great difficulty here. For some persons and institutions have a more or less clear and uncontested authority to *make* rules; and in such cases there exist, there are, those rules that they have made, provided of course that they have not been subsequently abrogated or – a less clear matter – allowed by desuetude to become a 'dead letter'. If I claim that your behaviour is in breach of some rule of, say, bridge, and you counter by denying that any such rule exists, it should be quite easy to settle that question conclusively; we consult the current edition of the official rule-book, and the rule in question either is in there or is not. Such a rule, to 'exist', need not always be complied with. Of course, if the authority of some rule-making body is contested, it might be held that it cannot and so does not really make *rules*; I shall not accept as *the* rules of, say, golf, or perhaps as rules at all, putative rules issued by some body whose authority in that field I do not acknowledge. But there may well, as we have seen, be undoubted rules of golf, made by uncontested authority, which nevertheless are seldom, or even perhaps never, complied with –

a great many, probably, of which most golfers are not even aware, but some also of which the ordinary player, in ordinary play, takes the reasonable view that he need not comply with them. In this sense one may 'accept' a rule – that is, admit that it *is* a rule and even that it is wholly proper that there should be that rule – and yet think, consistently and reasonably, that one need not comply with it.

Unfortunately, however, this simple part of the story is not the whole story. For it would be, though convenient, restrictive and unrealistic to hold that that only is a rule which is properly made by some authoritative rule-making body or person. We must admit, it seems, that there are rules which no rule-maker has ever made; and it is a separate question what the 'existence' of these consists in.

A separate question, and inevitably, it seems, a quite different sort of answer. A 'made' rule, as one might put it, has a way of 'existing' that is substantially independent of what people in general either think or do – namely, just by being made. If properly made, then there *is* that rule, even if people in general do not know that there is, or do not comply with it, or even do not think at all of their behaviour *as* either complying with the rule or contravening it. But an unmade rule does not have, *ex hypothesi*, that way of existing; and hence one may think that the existence of such a rule cannot be independent of what people think or do. For what else could its existence be a matter of? But if there is dependence here, how does it work out?

One might say this: there is reason to say that *there is* a certain rule, if certain behaviour could reasonably be held to be in compliance with or breach of that rule. The 'existence' of the rule might be, so to speak, presupposed in descriptions of, and in critical attitudes towards, certain behaviour; and in such a case to admit the 'existence' of the rule would be to 'accept' (whatever that means) the descriptions and critical attitudes which presuppose it.

We had better consider some cases. Is there, for example, in Western bourgeois circles, a rule that black bow ties are to be worn with dinner-jackets? I would be inclined to say there is not. Of course it is in some ways as if there were. There is, at any rate in some circles, a fairly uniform practice of wearing that sort of tie; and since it seems unplausible to say, and there is no apparent reason why it should be the case, that people just *prefer* to wear that sort of tie and regularly do so just for that reason, and since, generally speaking, they obviously *could* wear any sort of tie with a dinner-jacket, it is as if, in fairly regularly donning black bow ties, they were complying with a rule that such ties are to be worn. But then one might think that what they are complying with here is not really a *rule*; and the ground for so thinking (whether rightly or wrongly) would be, I suppose, that non-compliance does not evoke the right critical attitude. Roughly, one might think that a person wearing a red tie, or no tie at all, is unusually dressed, rather than *wrongly* dressed; his get-up is perhaps unconventional, but perhaps not *wrong*; and if so, one may think that what it deviates from is just a convention, or a custom, and not really a rule. I should suppose that the boundaries here are somewhat hazy; but it does seem reasonable to suggest that certain behaviour is not to be regarded as in breach of a *rule* if it simply is, and is simply regarded as, unusual; if it is to be said that there is a *rule*, then there must be some propensity to criticize adversely such behaviour as would constitute (assuming no special justification for it) a breach of the rule.

Does one, then, comply with a rule, if one 'regularly' acts in a certain manner with, in addition, the thought that people *should* so act? Plainly not, I think. Suppose for instance that, being of a very cautious disposition, I never venture out of doors in England without an umbrella, and perhaps think that both I and others ought never to do so; do I therein comply with a rule that one should always take an umbrella when going out of doors? I think not. In such a case it seems that taking an umbrella is simply something that I think there is always good reason to do; and in saying, for instance, why I judge adversely those who do not take umbrellas, I will mention what I take to be this ever-present good reason, without mention of anything that looks at all like a rule. Or consider the situation of the spectator of a cricket-match, ignorant of the game, and trying to work out what rules the players are following. He will find for instance that, when six balls have been bowled from one end, the players regularly move round and six balls are then bowled from the other end; deviations from this, he will observe, are adversely criticized. He will probably find also that, when a fast bowler is replaced by a slow one, some persons who were previously stationed quite close to the batsman are moved further away, some, probably, a lot further away; and he will find that, if this is not done, there is adverse criticism. But if he concludes that, in so acting, the players are following rules, he will of course be right in the first case, and wrong in the second. There is no *rule* that a slow bowler should not operate with exactly the same field-setting as a fast one; this is indeed scarcely ever done, and it would nearly always be regarded as wrong to do it, but that is because, quite independently of any rules, it is something which there is nearly always good reason not to do.

This fits, it seems to me, with a point we noticed earlier. There is, we said, no apparent need to *make* a rule, if there is reason to anticipate that people are anyway going to act as the rule, if superfluously made, would prescribe that they should do; so, at least very often, there will be no need to make a rule requiring that to be done which people will anyway see that there is good reason to do. This seems to fit well with what the last paragraph suggests – that is, that if people regularly act in a certain way because they think that there is always good reason to do so, then it will be inappropriate to say that they do so in compliance with a rule. For, somewhat as the making of a 'made' rule would be superfluous in such a case, so also would be the supposition that *there is* an 'unmade' rule; there is, so to speak, nothing in such a case for that supposition to do – that is, to account for.

It seems, then, that one might say something like this: a person is acting in compliance with a rule, and hence 'there is' that rule, *not* if he merely supposes, or it is supposed, that there is good reason regularly so to act, but rather if he supposes that he (or one) *is to* act in that way, *whether or not* in every case there is, there and then, good reason to do so. If, of course, he 'accepts' the rule, then he will presumably think that there is, in a general way, good reason for that to be done which the rule prescribes; but in complying with the rule here and now, he is not *merely* doing what he thinks, in the present case, there is good reason to do. Indeed, to hold that there is, and to be disposed to appeal to, a rule seems typically to involve the inclination as it were to

look away from the merits, if any, of the particular case; if I
think that there is a rule that ladies should take precedence of
men in going through doors and so on, then I do not raise the
question (special circumstances apart) why this lady here and
now should take precedence of me – I allow her to do so, since
that is what is to be done. I wear my medals above the left
breast-pocket of my tunic, not because I think they look particularly well there, but because that is where medals are to be
worn. Similarly, one might sometimes be tempted to allege that
there is a rule, precisely in the attempt to evade discussion of the
merits of a particular case; if I think that you should not, but are
unlikely to be able to see why you should not, wear your checked
yellow waistcoat when lunching with the Vice-Chancellor, I may
pretend there is a rule that only sober lounge-suits are to be worn
in that situation.

Two tricky questions need further consideration here. How is
the 'existence' of an unmade rule related, first, to compliance
with that rule, and second, to what may be called awareness of
it? Can there *be* such a rule with which, say, nobody complies?
And can there be such a rule, and can it be complied with or
broken, if those concerned are unaware of it, and do not *see*
their behaviour *as* either complying with a rule or failing to do
so?

On the first question, since it seems right to say in general that
any rule can be broken, one might at first be inclined to say that
of course there may always be a rule which everybody breaks.
Certainly, 'made' rules present no problem here; as mentioned
earlier, there may well be rules in, for instance, the official rule-
book of golf with which golfers seldom, or even never, comply.
But with unmade rules the question may arise how, if no appropriate rule-following behaviour ever occurs, one could
reasonably hold that the rule exists. Well, one may say, because
appropriate rule-*breaking* behaviour occurs. But what could
identify that behaviour *as* rule-breaking? It seems that the only
possible answer is: the attitudes of people towards that behaviour.
But then, of what people? And here one cannot, I think, do better
than say: of enough people, or perhaps, in some cases, of the
right people. Suppose that, in a certain royal court, no one –
perhaps because of the insignificant personality of the current

monarch – bothers to wait for the monarch to initiate conversation; it seems that it might still be said that there is a rule that people at court should do so, provided that enough of those concerned would concede that, strictly, the prevailing lax practice is not as it should be, or perhaps that a few courtiers regarded as of special authority on such questions would still maintain that there is such a rule, notwithstanding the present common neglect of it. But one should add, no doubt, that this would scarcely look like good sense if the putative rule had *never* been complied with, and also that, if general neglect were sufficiently protracted, it would be natural to regard the rule as, so to speak, gradually fading away. The time would surely come when it would seem reasonable to all but the most antiquarian to say that, while there used to be that rule for the conduct of courtiers, there is no such rule nowadays. Surely the critical attitudes of a single bigot would not be enough to sustain the existence of a rule.

But can one be following a rule, if one is unaware of doing so – a rule, perhaps, of whose very existence one is unaware? This is, in some connections, an issue of very great potential importance; but not, I believe, in this connection, so that, without too much fuss and trepidation, I suggest that one cannot. One could no more, I think, follow a rule of which one was unaware, than one could follow a route marked on a map which one has never seen. Of course, as I travel from Oxford to Aberystwyth, it may happen that I take the route marked, unknown to me, on your map; but in doing so I do not follow your map, nor fail to do so. Similarly, if I walk round the lawn on the gravel path, I may be doing what the rule – not to walk on the grass – prescribes; but I do not *obey* that rule, if I do not know of it, just as, if I do what the policeman told me to, I do not obey him if I could not hear, or could not understand, what he said to me. This point would perhaps seem too obvious to be worth making, if it were not that philosphers often seem to assume its denial; and this seems to be conspicuously so among philosophers of language. It may be the case that it would be possible in principle to express the grammar of, say, English in the form of a corpus of rules; it may even be the case, though it seems a much more extraordinary claim, that the meanings of English words and phrases might be expressed in the form of rules for their 'use' (more extra-ordinary, since it is deeply unclear what such rules would look like, or how there could be any determinate limit to their number). But that it might be possible to formulate such rules does not entail, though it seems often to be taken to, that there al-ready are such rules, and still less that those who speak and understand English are in fact following rules in doing so. It is admitted that, in some cases, no one yet knows what the sup-posed rules actually are, and it is certain that many who speak the language do not know. If so, then I think that it is only in some most unusual sense that they can be said, in speaking and construing the language, to be following rules – though to speak in this way is not, indeed, necessarily damagingly wrong, except perhaps in that it may tend to suggest that thereby lin-guistic performance has somehow been explained. But plainly it has not been; for linguistic competence is not, in any ordinary sense, familiarity with rules; and whether or not the strange sense in which it might be is at all explanatory, must await fur-ther specification of what that sense is and what is supposed to be explained. Of course, from the mere fact that competent speakers of, say, English produce the *right* words, or assign the *right* interpretation to what they read or hear, the existence of rules they have mastered does not immediately follow. For, clearly, it is not in general the case that what is 'right' is right in virtue of its conformity to some rule. It is right to attack one's steak with the sharp side of the knife rather than the blunt one, but not in virtue of a rule laying down how knives are to be used.

One more question: are rules essentially susceptible of de-liberate change? I believe that they are. Again, 'made' rules seem to present no problem here: for the authority of some person, or some body or institution, to make rules seems inseparable from, indeed practically to include, the authority to amend or rescind, qualify or supplement them. At any rate, rules that have been made by some deliberate act surely could in principle be abolished or changed in just the same way. But what of unmade rules? There is obviously the difficulty here that, since such a rule does not owe its existence to the act of any specifiable individual or institution, it is not clear by *whose* deliberate decision such a rule could be changed. But this appears to me to raise only a practical difficulty. For if such a rule is taken to owe its existence simply to its being 'accepted' or 'recognized' (not necessarily complied with in practice) by enough people, or by the right people, then it seems possible in principle, though perhaps not always in practice, for the rule to be changed by general agreement among those people. If for instance there has come to be, in a certain society, a recognized though unmade rule of etiquette to the effect that fish is to be eaten with a fork only, it would not be impossible for those concerned – fashionable hostesses, for instance, or even perhaps every member of the society – deliberately to agree to change this rule; to limit its scope, for instance, to certain kinds of fish, or even wholly to rescind its proscription of the useful fish-knife. No doubt this is unlikely – this is not in fact how such a rule is likely to change – but it is not impossible. So too, I think, for linguistic rules, if there really are such. If we suppose that, for instance, it was a rule of classical Greek that neuter plural substantives take the verb in the singular, then it seems that it would not have been conceptually impossible, though no doubt exceedingly difficult and improbable, for Greek speakers generally to have decided to drop that rule from some specified date. That a rule is not made by anyone's deliberate act does not imply that it cannot in that way be changed; there is an analogy here with, say, traditions and customs, which cannot perhaps be voluntarily instituted as from a particular moment, but which certainly can, at any time, be deliberately abandoned.

We embarked, it will be remembered, on this brisk survey of the notion of a rule, as a preliminary to the consideration of 'Rule-Utilitarianism' – the contention that morality *is*, at least in part, a system of rules, the general end of Utility constituting the *rationale*, not of particular morally right or wrong acts or at least not of all such, but rather of the rules themselves. Now this raises the issue: *are* there 'moral rules'? Is there any good reason to hold that there are such things? For of course, if there is not, the Rule-Utilitarian *theory* of morality cannot possibly be correct.

That there are moral rules, in *some* sense, seems readily admissible; namely, there are *made* rules. There are cases in which people have, or at any rate are taken to have, authority over other people of a sort that extends to concern for their moral well-being; and one way in which such authority may be exercised is in the making of rules on matters of morality, which it would seem quite natural to speak of as moral rules. I do not know whether it would be accurate to say that Popes actually do this, but it seems to be something that in principle a Pope could do; and it is often said, reasonably enough, that the moral education of children at any rate may include, at a certain stage, the promulgation to them by parents and teachers of rules for their conduct on certain moral matters, which also it would be natural to speak of as moral rules. It is perhaps by a sort of analogy with such cases that a person may be said to make moral rules for himself; though I may have no authority over the conduct of others, it seems that I could always 'make it a rule' for myself that I am or am not to do this or that; and sometimes such a rule would be a moral rule.

However, if it is admitted that there are moral rules in *this* sense, it must surely be added at once that they are of no great theoretical importance. For one thing, if there are such rules, that there are is in a sense accidental, or at any rate contingent. A man who has moral views about things, and who tries by and large to live up to his moral views, does not *necessarily* make *rules* (in this sense) for himself in seeking to do so. Somewhat as, if I think that it is always prudent to take an umbrella when going out of doors in England, I am not following a rule in regularly doing so, I may abstain from seeing, say, pornographic films, not because I have 'made it a rule' to keep away from such things, but merely because I regularly judge it to be morally wrong not to do so. I do not need, as it were, to make a rule, if I am anyway going to see, and to be duly moved by, moral reasons for doing what the rule would enjoin me to do. Similarly, the case for moral rules made by authority seems to rest only on the contingent fact that those for whom they are made *need* to be guided or sustained by rules. Children perhaps need rules because of their un-reason and inexperience, and the faithful perhaps because of their human frailty, or of the danger, in the absence of a 'ruling', of unsettling moral controversy.

But more important is the fact that, if there are moral rules in this sense, they must, so to speak, be non-fundamental. For behind such rules, as behind any rules, must be reasons for their existence. If there is a 'made' moral rule proscribing, say, the practice of contraception, then there is that rule for the reason that, in the judgement of the relevant rule-maker, the practice of contraception *is* morally wrong; and the fundamental question is then as to the merits of that judgement. The question of moral right or wrong cannot, so to speak, *stop* at any made rule, since the further question in this case – as to the merits of the rule – is itself a question about moral right or wrong. If there is any sense at all in which the 'making' of a moral rule could by itself *make* certain conduct morally wrong, this could be so only in the rather strained and feeble sense that it might be held to *be* morally wrong to disregard any rule whatever made by the authority concerned. But even here, it would be the merits of this latter notion that were really fundamental.

It seems clear enough, then, that if there are, as I anyway would be quite ready to admit that there are, moral rules *in this sense,* that there are such rules cannot be of any great importance in moral philosophy. For there *need* not be any such rules; and even if there are, they serve only to raise immediately the deeper question, whether what the rules prescribe or proscribe or license really *is* morally right or wrong or unobjectionable. But if so, it seems reasonable, even charitable, to suppose that philosophers who have spoken of moral rules as somehow essential or central in morality have not had in mind such rules as these; and that raises the question whether, in some other and less peripheral sense, there are moral rules. We had better reserve this large issue for another chapter.

5. Moral Rules

It is natural, I think, to entertain the idea that there are moral rules *somewhat* as, though of course not exactly as, there are legal rules. Bentham, in fact, first put forward his criterion of Utility as a standard for the appraisal, and where necessary reform, of systems of law; it was to determine the merits, that is, not of acts, but of rules. So one may think – as some of Bentham's successors certainly did think, though waveringly at times – that the problem of morality is an analogous problem; here too, there are rules, and the problem is that of determining their merits.[1]

Up to a point it is easy to see how one might be tempted by this idea. If one takes a broad, general look at the phenomenon of law, it seems possible to say something in a general way as to what legal systems are for, or what their point is – not necessarily what, in this particular case or that, their point actually is, but what, as one might say, it reasonably and justifiably would be. It seems that, in the first place, where you have large numbers of people living a more or less complicated social life, in which the doings and affairs of some cannot but affect and impinge upon and generally become involved with the doings and affairs of others, there will inevitably be vastly many transactions and relationships in which, if only to avoid confusion and uncertainty, *regulation* is needed. This, roughly, is the business of systems of 'civil' law. But though it is an important object, it is of course not the only object, of a legal system to, so to speak, smooth out or tidy up the interactions and inter-relations of those whose system it is; it is not the only object to stipulate how certain things are to be done which, in the absence of regulation,

<hr>

[1] This chapter, and parts of chapter 7 below, are derived from a paper of mine on which I have had the benefit of criticism by J. C. B. Gosling and many others; I recall particularly the philosophers of Sheffield, Newcastle, and Keele.

would tend to bog down in confusion and uncertainty. There is also, typically, the very different object of getting people to behave *better* than they would otherwise be liable to do; it is another object of the legal system to exert a certain pressure against what are taken to be objectionable ways of behaving, and correspondingly in favour or support of desirable ways. To this different end, then, certain *rules of law* are made and promulgated, or very often are merely recognized and maintained in practice, laying down that actions of certain specified kinds are (for instance) not to be done; and, in order to make such rules effective for their purpose, provision is made for the detection, formal investigation, and punishment of non-compliance with them.

Now what seems to be tempting, and understandably so, is to think of 'morality' as partially, but importantly, analogous with a legal system in this latter respect. It seems and is, after all, completely reasonable to say that the object or end of morality, as in part of law, is to bring it about that people behave better than they would otherwise be liable to do, or to exert a certain pressure, for instance, against what are taken to be objectionable ways of behaving; and it perhaps is natural enough, having got so far, to go on to think that, as law pursues this end by calling for compliance with rules, so does morality. Of course, certain differences leap immediately to the eye. The rules of morality, moral rules, are not (except, as we have noted, peripherally) formally *made*, as rules of law often are, by any authoritative rule-making person or body; they must presumably be thought of rather, perhaps like the rules of some games, as being simply informally *recognized* by those whose conduct they are to guide and influence. Again, there is, except in so far as the law itself may intervene, no formal institution of detection, trial, and punishment; the rules are to operate, as it is sometimes put, 'internally', not by way of merely external enforcement. Nevertheless, one may think that, as the law is in part a formally made and enforced system of rules whose object is to get people to behave better than they might otherwise do, so morality is to be thought of as a system of rules with the very same object, though indeed not made or administered in at all the same way. Law and morals, some would say, are both to be seen as 'instruments of social control', both requiring – if not necessarily securing – compliance with rules: it is just that the one instrument is more formalized, institutionalized, and more 'external' than the other.

But this comparison, if we dwell on it further, runs into some difficulties. Suppose that in some community, for instance in our own, there is a rule of law against driving motor vehicles at high speeds, for instance over 30 m.p.h., in certain specified areas. We may say, intelligibly enough, that the existence of that rule *makes* speeding in those areas illegal, a legal offence. It does not, however, make such conduct objectionable. It may indeed make it marginally more objectionable than it would otherwise be, since some, as we have seen, might think it objectionable in itself, in at least some degree, to break any rules properly made and promulgated by the authorities of one's community; but quite apart from that, it is obviously objectionable anyway, and specifically dangerous, to drive motor vehicles very fast where there is a high-ish chance of people being in the way of them. (No doubt, if I *just* exceed the specified limit, my behaviour is not in that case *very* objectionable; there is a question of degree here, but let us ignore that complication). Thus, in this very typical sort of case, we have a certain sort of conduct, namely fast driving in populous areas, *made* illegal, by the framing and promulgation of a suitable rule, precisely because, antecedently to and independently of the rule, that sort of conduct is already taken to *be* objectionable. It is not taken to be illegal; it is made illegal. But it is not made objectionable; it is taken to be objectionable anyway. Its being illegal might be said to be the 'effect' of the rule; but its being objectionable is not the 'effect' of any rule, but is rather the reason for making the rule in the first place. If there were no such rule, that sort of conduct would not be illegal; but it would still, in virtue of being dangerous, be (usually) objectionable.

Turn now to the case of a 'moral rule'. Let us suppose for the sake of argument that there is a moral rule against, say, contraception. Well, if there is, the question seems to arise: does the existence of that rule *make* the practice of contraception morally wrong? Or does the rule rather proscribe the practice because it is, antecedently and independently, taken to *be* morally wrong?

One encounters here straight off, it seems to me, a certain perplexity as to how to understand these supposed alternatives. If asked 'Does this rule of law against speeding *make* speeding illegal, or does it rather proscribe what is anyway taken to *be* illegal?', one can readily answer: 'Well, if there were no such rule, of course speeding would still be objectionable; but there would then be no basis for calling it *illegal*. Therefore, the rule does actually *make* it illegal; without the rule it would not be illegal, though objectionable no doubt'. Correspondingly, if asked 'Does the moral rule against contraception *make* it morally wrong?', one feels inclined to begin 'Well, if there were no such rule . .'. But then one may well wonder: what does that *mean*?

Well, what could it mean? The general notion that we are considering is, let us recall, that morality is to be regarded as a system of rules somewhat resembling a legal system, with however the conspicuous difference (no doubt among others) that its rules are not formally made, or administered or enforced, by any authoritative persons or institutions. If so, then the 'existence' of the rules in the system will presumably have to be regarded as a matter of their informal 'recognition' by those concerned. This, as emerged, I take it, in the last chapter, does not seem to be an impossible idea in itself. I take it, for example, that cricket was played long before the M.C.C., or any comparable authority, formally codified and announced the rules of cricket; and it does not seem outrageous to say that, in those early, unregimented days, there still *were* rules of cricket – rules, certainly not authoritatively made and published nor perhaps even formulated, but just generally 'recognized' in a friendly, informal sort of way by people playing cricket. In such a case, 'if there were no such rule . .' would mean 'if, in their conduct, criticism of the conduct of others, and so on, those concerned did not so act as to 'recognize' such a rule . .'. If, for instance, in the early, unregimented days of cricket, batsmen did not hesitate to prevent straight deliveries from hitting their stumps by interposing their legs, and if nobody ever protested, or claimed that they should leave the scene, when they did so, we could say that *there was*, in those days, no l.b.w. rule; and of course, if there was, if in the conduct of the game such a rule was 'recognized', we could still consider hypothetically how things would have been, if there had been no such rule. This is fairly plain sailing.

So back now to the supposed moral rule against contraception. The phrase, puzzling at first sight, 'If there were no such rule . .', seems to be thus construable: 'If in their conduct, criticism of the conduct of others, and so on, those concerned did not (informally) 'recognize' such a rule . .'. The question we were to consider was: does the moral rule against the practice of contraception *make* it morally wrong? Alternatively put: is the moral wrongness of this practice *a matter of* its being contrary to a moral rule? And it now seems that this is to be understood as the question: if, in their conduct, criticism of the conduct of others, and so on, people did not (informally) recognize a rule proscribing contraception, would that practice, or would it not, *be* morally wrong?

This, however, is *not* plain sailing. For there appear to be two possible answers to this question, neither of which looks at all attractive. Consider, first, the possibility that being morally wrong is like being illegal – that is, that, just as something's being illegal is a matter of its being a breach of some legal rule, so something's being morally wrong is a matter of its being a breach of some moral rule. If so, then, just as something illegal would not *be* illegal if the legal rule in question did not exist, so something morally wrong would not *be* morally wrong if the moral rule in question did not exist. But it seems that this last phrase means, a bit abbreviatedly, 'if those concerned did not recognize such a rule . .'; and so this answer seems to yield the queer implication that morally wrong practices would actually not be morally wrong, if those concerned did not recognize moral rules proscribing them. But this seems to make the question, whether X is morally wrong, wholly a matter of the way people think about X. Rather as, in the early days of cricket, to defend your stumps with your legs could have been said to be against a rule of cricket only if those concerned agreed in thinking that it was and proceeding accordingly, so, on this view, the use, say, of torture could be said to be morally wrong only if those concerned should agree in thinking that it was and proceeding accordingly. But this, I take it, is not to most tastes at all a palatable conclusion: one might very naturally be inclined to insist that the use of torture, or the practice of contraception, just *is* morally wrong, or at any rate either is or not, whatever those concerned may be agreed in thinking about it.

I ought, I suppose, slightly to qualify this proposition by taking note of the fact, quite often important, that what people think of, how they regard, some form of behaviour can indeed be *relevant* to whether it is morally right or wrong for them, or for others, to behave in that way. If you believe that contraception is morally wrong, I may think you morally blameworthy in practising it, even if I myself think it morally unobjectionable; if I think that promiscuous sex is morally unobjectionable, I may still think it, and it may be, morally wrong for me to inveigle into that pursuit one who is firmly convinced of its moral wrongness. But although what people think is thus sometimes relevant, and sometimes crucially so, it still seems extremely paradoxical to suggest that the wrongness *in general* of some way of behaving could consist solely in people's viewing it in a certain manner. There is nothing 'wrong' in stopping straight balls with one's legs *except* that one is held to be 'out' if one does so; but could there be, in something that *is* morally wrong, nothing wrong *except* that it is held to be so?

But now, *this* point at least appears to be taken care of by the other possible answer. Let us try the idea that being morally wrong is to be compared, not with being illegal, but with being objectionable – the idea, that is, that something's being morally wrong is *not* just a matter of its being a breach of some moral rule, but rather that it is (if it is) 'recognized as' a breach of some moral rule just because it is taken to *be* morally wrong anyway. In that case we could say that, just as driving very fast in built-up areas just *is* objectionable (because dangerous), whether or not there is a rule making it actually illegal, so the use of torture, say, just *is* morally wrong, whether or not people recognize it as a breach of a moral rule. Its *being* morally wrong, if so, would not come out as wholly dependent on the way people think about it; and we have escaped the unpalatable conclusion of the foregoing paragraph.

Well, yes: but if we seek to escape the unpalatable conclusion in this way, we do so at the price of substantially undermining the initial, rather tempting partial assimilation of morality to law, and indeed of making *this* sort of talk of moral rules look empty and redundant.

Consider again the case of fast driving in populous areas. We say, for fairly obvious reasons, that this is, as a practice, objectionable; specifically, it constitutes a danger to life and limb. It is, moreover, perfectly possible for people in general to appreciate that this is so, and it is even quite likely that some drivers of vehicles might be moved by such appreciation to moderate their speed. Nevertheless, a legal *rule* against speeding may still be desiderated, and its existence may still make a substantial difference; for the introduction of such a rule brings in a whole vast consequential apparatus of prevention, scrutiny, detection, and punishment, which may well induce to behave as they should in this respect those who, if merely left to work out for themselves that fast driving in built-up areas is objectionable, would either not do so, or not bother to moderate their speed accordingly.

But now turn back to the moral case. On the view just described, contraception, say, is just taken to *be* morally wrong, much as speeding in built-up areas just *is* objectionable; and if it is, one would think it reasonable to suppose that people in general might be capable of appreciating that that is so, and might even be disposed to regulate their conduct accordingly. But if so, what is supposed to be the role of 'moral rules'? They do not, on this view, figure in the *conceptual* role of elucidating what it *is* for something to be morally wrong; for on this view something, say contraception, can *be* morally wrong antecedently to, and whether or not 'there is', a moral rule proscribing its use. But if they do not come in in that way, what reason is there to bring them in at all? The 'existence' of a moral rule would not, as does the existence of a legal rule, bring in any special formal procedures of detection and deterrence; in the supposition that there is a moral rule against the practice of contraception there is, so to speak, nothing to deter or deflect a person from that practice that is not already present in the appreciation, if he has it, that the practice itself is morally wrong. He might, indeed, be given pause by the anticipation, or awareness, of unfavourable critical attitudes in others. But such critical attitudes need not be seen as evoked by – indeed, as partially constituting – the breach of a *rule*; for they are, one would suppose, just as capable of being evoked by conduct which is taken to *be* morally wrong. In the legal case, there is a very clear difference between my thinking that a certain sort of conduct is objectionable, and that it is contrary to a rule of law; I may, in thinking it objectionable, see reason, and be actually inclined, to avoid so acting, but I have in any case an *extra* reason, in thinking it illegal. But in the moral case, if I think that certain conduct is morally wrong, it is not clear what difference could be supposed to be made by the supposition that it is contrary to a moral *rule*.

What has gone wrong here? It seems to me that what has gone wrong is simply that we have been trying to make work a misconceived analogy. Let me put it in this way. In the case of a legal system, a system of rules of law, it is possible to make a quite clear and intelligible distinction between what might be called the 'effect' of the rules, and the 'basis' of the rules. We have, as the basis of the rules, or at any rate of a lot of them, the *view* that certain sorts of conduct are, say, undesirable and ought to be discouraged – that, for instance, it is undesirable that vehicles should be driven at high speeds in populous areas. If now rules are actually made, or at any rate recognized and enforced, on this basis, we can clearly distinguish the 'effect' of such rules. That effect is partly conceptual – it is now possible to characterize certain sorts of conduct, for instance speeding in populous areas, in a new way, namely as *illegal*; and partly practical – in consequence of the rule, certain special processes of detection, deterrence, and (if necessary) punishment are brought into play, which are meant to make, and doubtless do make, a practical difference, a difference in what actually happens. Notice particularly that this does *not* depend on the supposition that rules of law are formally and explicitly *made*: even if, for instance in some comparatively primitive society, or in some system in which formal legislation plays a minor part, the 'existence' of most or all legal rules were a matter merely of their informal recognition by those concerned, it would still be possible thus to distinguish the 'effect', conceptual and practical, of the rules, from the 'basis' of the rules – from, that is, the non-legal, or pre-legal, views about conduct to which the rules are intended to 'give effect'. But in the case of morality none of this makes any sense. We have, no doubt, something corresponding to what we have called the 'basis' of legal rules – that is, *views* which people hold, to the effect that certain sorts of conduct are, for example, morally wrong. But if we then seek to bring in rules, in some sort of putative analogy with legal rules, it is evident, I think, that this move is really idle, adds nothing, makes no difference. For such supposititious rules would have absolutely no 'effect'. If I believe that, say, contraception is morally wrong, I am not in a position to characterize it in any *new* way if I suppose it to be a breach of a 'moral rule'; for that is, if anything, just to say again that it is morally wrong. Similarly, if it is taken to be morally wrong, nothing different *happens* if it is held to be a breach of a 'moral rule'; the idea that certain conduct was in breach of a 'moral rule' might indeed have practical consequences, but they could only be exactly the same consequences as would follow from its being taken to be morally wrong. In a nutshell: rules of law are distinguishable from, and 'give effect' to, views people have about what is, for instance, objectionable in conduct. But supposed 'moral rules' would not 'give effect' to people's moral views; to talk about them is just a misleading way of talking about those views themselves. To bring rules in – at any rate in this way – is to add nothing but a quite substantial risk of confusion.

It seems, however, that the idea of 'moral rules' is not wholly parasitic upon this sort of putative analogy with law; so that we are not yet finished with it. I have been arguing so far that the institution, or 'existence', of a rule of law is, sometimes anyway, a way of 'giving effect' to *views* people have on what is desirable or otherwise in social conduct – views which are in a sense independent of the rule, and which provide its 'basis'. People might, that is, hold, and when appropriate express and act on, such views, whether or not there were an actual rule to give effect to them (though perhaps we should take note here that, where there is a rule, it may sometimes, in a sort of feed-back fashion, serve to maintain, and even reinforce, the views that lie behind it); and the views that people hold form an important part of the *reason* that could be given for having the rule, and for having *that* rule. Rules of this sort, then, conspicuously rules of law, could be said – along with, often, attendant procedures of enforcement – to constitute a kind of institutional superstructure upon, and over and above, the views people hold. But morality, I have suggested, is not an *institution* in that sense; it is not a superstructure of rules over and above, and having as its basis, moral views to which it somehow gives institutionalized 'effect'. It is not – as I mentioned in the last chapter – that there *could* not be 'moral' rules in this sense; indeed, where there is some suitably recognized moral *authority*, such as a Pope or a parent, there might well be some such rules, and probably are. But rules in this sense are not, so to speak, the essence of the case; if there are such, they are neither essential nor fundamental.

However, now we must ask: what is it to 'hold a moral view'? Perhaps there need not be rules *over and above* moral views; but may there not be rules, so to speak, involved *in* moral views? Perhaps to hold such a view just *is* to recognize a rule; and if so, while perhaps there are not or need not be 'superstructural' rules, there will be ground-floor rules involved *in* holding moral views.

How could this be? Well, the suggestion might be, I suppose, that to think something X, say, morally wrong just *is* to accept the rule, say, 'Never X', or 'No X-ing', or 'X-ing not allowed'. (One might, presumably, 'accept' such a rule, as one certainly does others, without necessarily supposing that there could absolutely never be proper, or justified, exceptions made to it; indeed, one scarcely could sensibly suppose this, since there would doubtless be more than one such rule, and where there are two rules or more, rules may conflict). Now, it may look at first sight as if this suggestion can be easily rejected, and is even absurd. For surely, if I am sensibly to accept a rule 'Never X', I must have some reason for accepting it – for accepting a rule at all, and specifically *that* rule; but – if the rule is to be said to be a *moral* rule – what could that reason possibly be except the *view* that to X is, actually, morally wrong? But if so, to hold that view cannot *be* to accept that rule; to hold the view is to have a *reason for* accepting the rule. But if that is right, why should accepting the *rule* come in at all? What would it come in for? For surely I may hold, and express and act upon, the view *itself*, leaving nothing – as we put it once before – for the supposed 'rule' to do.

This, however, can scarcely be conclusive of the question. For the suggestion we are considering can be reduced to absurdity in this way only if we make the supposition that the reason for accepting the moral rule 'Never X' must be the view that to X is, actually, morally wrong; for if that is so, and only if that is so, it immediately follows that to hold that view cannot simply *be* to accept that rule. But what if the reason for accepting the rule is something else? Then, since 'having a reason' would not *be* holding the moral view, it might still be that holding that view was a matter of accepting the rule that one has some (other) reason to accept.

Let us go at this, for brevity, in a bald and formal fashion. Suppose that I take some species of conduct X to have some feature or property Q – where we need not go further into the question what Q is than to stipulate that it shall *not* be the 'property' of being morally wrong. Suppose further that I regard the fact that X is Q as a good reason for there being, for accepting, a rule against X-ing. Now, it might be suggested, to take X to be morally wrong perhaps *is* to accept, for the reason that X is Q, a 'No X-ing' *rule*. This version is not patently absurd, as the former one was. What are we to make of it?

Well, one may still wonder here why a rule should come into it. We have not tried to specify what sort of property Q, in this blue-print, might be. We have, however, supposed – in fact we brought it in for just that purpose – that the fact that some species of conduct X is Q is, or at least could intelligibly be taken as, a reason for a rule against X-ing; but – one may say – if the fact that X is Q is taken to be a reason for a rule against X-ing, then surely it must be taken to be a reason for not X-ing *anyway*. (The fact that smoking in the ammunition store is dangerous is not merely a reason for accepting a rule against smoking; it is also a reason for *not smoking*). And if so, once again, what is there for the rule to do? Why, if someone thinks that there is reason of a certain sort for not X-ing, could that not *itself* be for him to hold the view that to X is morally wrong? Why should we suppose that, thinking that there is such a reason, he must, so to speak, go further, and accept a *rule*? What *is* 'going further' anyway? What difference does it make?

Well, it does not, I think, make no difference at all; and what the difference is, may emerge from the following example. Suppose that I hold a certain view about cricket – a practical view, a view as to what should be done, what is the right thing to do;

namely, I hold the view that, at the start of an innings, the captain of the fielding side should use his faster bowlers. Suppose furthermore that I act accordingly – when I am captain in such a case I put on my faster bowlers, if other captains do not do so I express, or conceivably repress, adverse criticism, if asked for advice I give *that* advice, and so forth. Now there is absolutely no need here to talk about a *rule*. Of course it is not a rule of cricket that the fast-ish men are to open the bowling; but nor is it, in any sense, a rule of my own. For why do I hold this view, and act in this way? I hold the view that one should open with fast-ish bowlers because there is (I think) good reason to do just that (unsettled batsmen, shine on the ball, and so on); and I act accordingly whenever occasion arises because, on each such occasion, there is, and I see, good reason so to act. In all this there is nothing for reference to a rule to do – that is, nothing that calls for description or explanation in such a way. My view, and my actions, criticisms, advice, and so on are sufficiently accounted for by the reasons for so acting that, in general, there are, and that there are in particular on each occasion when the issue comes up. And it is worth noting here that, if I hold this sort of view in the way outlined, you could doubtless get me to agree that it is at least conceivable that a case might arise in which it would *not* be right for a captain to act in that way; for if, as I hold, a captain should act in that way for certain statable reasons on each occasion, it will doubtless be at least conceivable that a case should arise in which either there are not those reasons, or there are more cogent reasons for acting in some other way. Perhaps a few opening batsmen are peculiarly vulnerable to leg-spin, or a few fast-ish bowlers rather weak in handling a new ball; or perhaps one has to let the Duke of Edinburgh open the bowling.

Now, how exactly would the case be different, if a *rule* were involved? Consider, for a start, an actual rule of cricket – say that six balls, and no more, are to be delivered from each end in turn. Now there is doubtless good reason for having *some* rule on that matter, though it is perhaps a bit arbitrary that we have exactly that rule. (Two deliveries per over would no doubt be too few, and ten too many, but, as Aristotle might have observed, it does not follow that the mean-point, six, must be exactly right.) But, even if there is good reason for having just that rule, umpires do not, on each occasion when bowlers have bowled six balls, bring the over to an end because they see, on each occasion, good reason to do so. There are in fact plenty of cases in which, from the batsman's or bowler's or even spectator's point of view, it would be an excellent thing to have more than six balls; but the fact is that the *merits* of such cases do not come into it. The rule specifies in advance, in general but wholly unambiguous terms, that exactly six balls and no more *are to* be delivered; and umpires see to it that such is actually done, not because on each occasion there is good reason to do that, but because there is a rule prescribing that that *is to* be done. The question, whether or not it would, in the circumstances, be a good thing to carry on after six balls are bowled, is not to arise, or at any rate not except as a matter of non-practical speculation. What the rule does, in fact, is to *exclude* from practical consideration the particular merits of particular cases, by specifying in advance what *is to* be done, whatever the circumstances of particular cases may be. And similarly, if, though it is not of course a rule of cricket, I were as captain to 'make it a rule' for myself that my fast-ish bowlers are to bowl first, this would be, so to speak, to resolve in advance that just that *is to* be done, without regard to the particular merits of particular cases. The captain who holds the view that the fast men should bowl first, and the captain who 'makes it a rule' that they should, of course may act in just the same way – each may open the bowling, every time, with his faster bowlers. But it is not in the same way, so to speak, that they come to do so. The one man, whatever the exact situation may be, follows his rule that that is what is to be done; the other man considers each situation as he finds it, and regularly sees reason to act in that way in each case. If one asked them why, one would get different answers, notwithstanding that what they do is exactly the same.

We see, then, what is done by the intrusion of a rule. The 'effect' of the rule is that, in the cases in which it applies, it is specified in advance what *is to* be done; that question is removed from the sphere of judgement on the particular merits of each case. We have already foreshadowed this conclusion, it may be remembered, in the course of our earlier general consideration of rules.

So, then: does rule-acceptance come into the holding of moral views? Well, if this were taken to be a question about moral psychology, an empirical question concerning what actually goes on, then I take it the answer must be that it sometimes does. That is, there probably are people, perhaps very many, who, supposing that there is some reason Q for not X-ing, do 'make it a rule' never to X; if ever a situation comes up when in principle they could X, they take actually doing so to be simply 'ruled out'; without very much, perhaps even without any, appraisal of the pros and cons, in just this situation, of doing this or that, they write off, as simply not to be done, any course of action which they recognize, in general, as a case of X-ing. That this, as a matter of individual psychology in some cases, perhaps in many, does actually occur, I take to be undeniable.

But *should* it occur? Is this part, so to speak, of the Idea of morality, as opposed to being merely a feature of its empirical realizations in certain cases? This is a question not altogether easy to answer.

It is tempting, and I think ultimately right, to say that it should *not* occur. For to 'follow a rule', as we have seen, is, at any rate in this sort of case, as it were to turn away from consideration of the particular merits of particular cases; and it does not appear that, in the sphere in which moral judgement is exercised, there is any particular consideration to justify doing so. Of course, in other cases there may be such considerations – which is only to say, after all, that to have, and to follow, rules is not always a defect in rationality. Officials under a legal system follow rules, partly perhaps in order that there shall be some measure of uniformity in the way they operate, but more importantly because their operations are liable substantially to involve the position and interests of other persons, for whom it is highly desirable that such liability should be, so far as it can be, determinate and predictable. Sometimes, as perhaps in the apportionment of benefits to individuals by a public authority, the authority's functionaries will be required to follow definite rules, partly again for uniformity, partly to lessen the chance of improper discrimination, and partly – sometimes perhaps most crucially – to speed up their transaction of business. Then I might make rules for, say, the subordinates in my office, simply because I do not regard them as competent to make their own assessments of the merits of cases. In the sphere of moral judgement, however, there seem to be, in general, no relevant considerations of this sort. There is no special need, as in the case of public, legal or political institutions, for uniformity and predictability of operation; there is no need always, though indeed there may be sometimes, for expeditiousness; and, though I might make 'moral rules' for others, for example children, whom I do not regard as competent to judge for themselves, it could scarcely be for *this* reason that I might 'make rules' for myself – for how, if I need them for this reason, could I claim competence to decide what rules to make?[1] Thus one may think that, if the exercise of moral judgement, the holding of moral views, is to be the reasonable affair which it is surely ideally supposed to be, there should not occur any simplifying, undiscriminating, rather child-like acceptance of rules; for there is nothing to make such acceptance really reasonable. Rather, there should occur the constantly repeated attempt to achieve the best judgement on the full concrete merits of each individual case. One should thus consider what there is reason to do or not do, or what view there is reason to take, rather than, less discriminatingly, what is required by some rule, or permitted or ruled out by some rule.

I think that this will seem wrong to some people – and even perhaps, to some, repulsively wrong. It might be urged by some that the really morally good man is not one who, after more or less careful, Aristotelian deliberation, concludes that there is reason, say, not to act in a certain way, but one to whom it never occurs to act in that way – for whom, say, perjury, or the deliberate betrayal of a trust, are never seriously considered courses of action at all, but 'ruled out' as soon as recognized. Is there not, some would further urge, something even repulsive in supposing

---

[1] There is a possible answer to this rhetorical question. Might I not be well able, with the help of course of traditional wisdom and public opinion, to grasp what *kinds* of acts are *likely* to be, say, morally wrong, while being unable ever to be really sure of the actual moral merits of particular cases? And if so, would it not be reasonable for me to make it a *rule*, say, never to do particular acts of the kind that are *likely* to be morally wrong? Here rules would come in, not indeed as *constituting* the moral merits of particular cases, but as remedies for our inability to be sure what those merits are. G. E. Moore, I think, took this position in *Principia Ethica*; but I think that he also very considerably exaggerated the difficulty of determining what the moral merits of cases actually are.

that one must *have a reason* for not, say, shooting the prisoners one
has captured in battle, or assaulting, say, participants in a legal
and non-violent demonstration? What sort of person would it
be who *needed* a reason for not doing things of this sort?

One must not at this point, however, become over-excited.
It may be that, in most cases, the really morally good man does
not seriously consider, say, perjury or betrayal as possible courses
of action; perhaps, usually, it just never occurs to him to act in
those ways, or even to think about doing so. But, on the one
hand, it seems entirely reasonable to suppose that this may be
because he sees, at once and without difficulty, reason not so to
act – we do not need a *rule* to account for his deciding as, and so
unhesitatingly as, he does; and, on the other hand, it is not,
surely, completely obvious that there could not be cases in which
reasons *for* so acting should be seriously weighed. (Should the
first Duke of Marlborough not even have *considered*, in Novem-
ber 1688, whether or not to transfer his services to William of
Orange?) Similarly, it is perhaps repulsive to 'need a reason' for,
say, not shooting prisoners of war, if this implies that at first
sight one sees nothing much against it, and needs to be persuaded
into treating them with reasonable humanity. But though one
may not, and doubtless should not, need a reason in that way, it
does not follow that there *is* not a reason for not shooting them –
that that course is 'ruled out' by something *other* than a reason;
nor that, if I treat them decently, I may not quite allowably have a
reason for doing so.

I suggest then, that to hold moral views, to make moral judgements and moral decisions and so on, is not appropriately to be
regarded as a matter of accepting and applying moral *rules*; and
hence I would conclude that Rule-Utilitarianism is to be regarded
as, in a sense, a theory without any actual subject-matter. It
might, I suppose, be put forward as a recommendation – as
proposing that morality ought to be essentially a system of
rules, and that, secondly, the merits of such systems should be
assessed by the criterion of Utility; but as such it would, in my
judgement, not be persuasive, since, whatever may be the proper
criterion by which to assess the merits of systems of rules, I do
not see how the claim could be substantiated that morality
ought to be essentially such a system. One might also advance

the theory, I suppose, quite hypothetically, as a theory concerning assessment of the merits of moral rules, if any such there were; but it is not clear what would be interesting in that hypothetical exercise. What *is* rather interesting, I think, is the apparent fact that, if one does not mis-identify what is often taken to be the theory's subject-matter, it must turn out to be really identical with the simple, bald-headed version of Utilitarianism, considered and rejected much earlier, on which it was supposed to be a substantial improvement.[1] It seems to me that this must be so, for the following reason. If one considers the sorts of things which are likely to be put forward as specimens of the rules to which the theory of Rule-Utilitarianism is to apply, one finds, in my opinion, that they are not really rules at all, but general *propositions*. That lying is morally wrong, for example, or that undertakings given ought to be kept, is not a rule; it does not say that this or that is or is not to be done, but that something *is so*; it invites, not approval or disapproval of a rule, but assent or denial. (I am aware that the hackles of many philosophers will rise at this. If one calls it a *proposition* that lying is morally wrong, does that not imply that it could, at least in principle, be *true*? And if that proposition were true, would it not then be a *fact* that lying was morally wrong? And is it not agreed on all hands that there are no moral facts? I shall return to these well-worn, even thread-bare issues in chapter VIII, below; for the present, I ask only to be allowed to call that a proposition which, being expressible in the indicative mood, can also be said to be so or not so, be affirmed or denied, and also – as a matter of fact – be quite unsurprisingly called true or false.) But now, if what we have here are really not rules but a sort of propositions, is it not the thesis of Rule-Utilitarianism that the justification of, the ultimate ground of, all such propositions is set forth in the single standard or 'end' of Utility? But then – since it is not easy to see how one could argue that general moral propositions have grounds quite *different* from those of particular moral propositions – it looks as though this must lead directly to the contention that *all* propositions in morals have, ultimately, one

[1] A contention amounting to much the same as this one, though advanced on rather different and more elaborately argued grounds, is put forward by David Lyons in *Forms and Limits of Utilitarianism* (O.U.P., 1965).

and the same ground, namely Utility; and that is the thesis of simple Utilitarianism. The idea that the two versions of Utilitarianism are really different rests crucially, I think, on the supposition that the Rule version really is a doctrine about *rules* – that is, about something logically quite heterogeneous with particular moral judgements about this or that. If this is not so – if the elements, so to speak, of the theory are really *not* rules but a sort of judgements or propositions – then we must, I think, end up with just one doctrine here, rather than two – one doctrine, specifically, about the unique ground of moral propositions in general.

But it is time to move on. In this chapter, and in the one before it, I have made liberal use of the notion of *reasons*. I have distinguished rules from reasons for there being rules, and for there being *those* rules. I have distinguished acting in compliance with a rule from simply doing what one thinks that there is reason to do. I have distinguished thinking that there is good reason not to act in a certain way from thinking that to act in that way is 'ruled out' by a rule. And in effect I have suggested that to hold moral views, and when appropriate to express and to act on moral views, is not to be thought of as 'recognizing' or 'accepting' a system of rules, but rather as recognizing some range or variety of reasons for judging and, when appropriate, for saying or doing. It is this notion of reasons that now falls to be investigated.

6. Moral Virtues

In the second chapter of this book I raised the question: what is the apparatus of moral evaluation *for*? What is it supposed to do? If one were asked why it was worth going in for, what should be one's answer? I ventured there the very vague and general proposition (difficult, I believe, but doubtless by no means impossible, to disagree with) that the general object of the exercise – of moral evaluation of oneself or of others, of one's own acts or other people's, of past, present, future, or merely hypothetical acts – must be 'to contribute in some respects, by way of the actions of rational beings, to the amelioration of the human predicament'; and I went on to sketch out, in that same chapter, some of the 'limitations' inherent in the human predicament in virtue of which things are liable to go rather badly, and consequently to stand in need of amelioration. It is to this topic that, in search of illumination of the notion of 'moral reasons', I now want to return. For it seems evident that what, from the moral point of view, can be reasons to commend or condemn, to do or to abstain from doing, for both judgement and action, must be some function of what moral evaluation is supposed to achieve, of the end in view, and of the *way* in which it is supposed to achieve it; and this is an issue on which we have not yet found much to say that seemed at all satisfactory. We have rejected the idea that morality is supposed to work by proposing, in opposition to the native egoism of the unregenerate human, the single, simple injunction of universal beneficence; and we have rejected also the idea that it is supposed to work by requiring compliance with an – itself supposedly beneficent – system of rules. So now we need, in a sense, to re-open the question. There are certain very general facts about the human predicament, including certain very general facts about human beings, which seem to be reasonably regarded as setting up, in ways already briefly sketched, an inherent liability for things to go rather badly; what then, let us ask, is required, if things are to go better – or rather if, as by and large is the case, they are not actually to go quite so badly as they seem inherently liable to do? And where, among such requirements, might morality be seen as fitting in?

One might begin by saying that, if things are to go better in the sense in question – if, that is, people's needs and interests, and some at least of their wants, are to be more fully satisfied than they otherwise might be – one very basic *desideratum* would surely be greater resources from which to satisfy them. This is obviously true in a sense; but it is as well to be clear in what sense. Leaving on one side the tricky but scarcely relevant question of 'creative' thought, whether in the arts or elsewhere, we may tritely observe that human beings do not have the god-like faculty of absolute creation. In all our undertakings we must make do, in one way or another, with what there is; we cannot add to the stock of what there is *ex nihilo*. Thus the case is that, in the relevant sense, increasing the resources available for the satisfaction of people's needs, wants, and interests is a matter of making better use for that purpose of the resources, in a more basic sense, which are already available but cannot be increased by our own efforts. It is a matter, one might say, of turning unusable resources into usable ones, or of putting what there is into usable forms. And if that is to be done, one thing that is obviously and essentially required is knowledge – in the first place information about the environment, its contents and potentialities, and in the second place the vast variety of technical skills involved in its transformation into usable forms. Such knowledge must be acquired, preserved, disseminated, and transmitted.

Continuing at the same level of monstrous generality, one might mention next the obvious need for organization. It is perfectly obvious that very little of any sort would ever be done, if every individual attempted to do everything on his own, or merely in such more or less fortuitous groups as might be formed *ad hoc* from time to time by individual initiative. For vastly many purposes, the long-run co-operation of many individuals is absolutely necessary; and if such co-operation is to be effective, it must be somehow directed – there must be some way of determining objectives, and of regulating more or less closely what the roles of individuals are to be in the co-operative undertaking. It is of course largely at any rate from this necessity that there come to exist what may generally be called 'institutions' – tribes, national states, federations of states, clubs, associations and parties of all kinds, firms, trade unions, armies, universities, the Mafia, and so on. It need not be maintained that the formation and character of such more or less co-operative institutions is fully determined by strictly practical ends; some may be in part just 'natural', like the family perhaps in its more general aspects, though not in details, and some may be wholly or in part, as one might say, for fun, for the sake of the pleasures of association in itself. But that there *is* a practical necessity here is indisputable; there are countless things that we want and need that we could not possibly get, even if it were known how they could be got, without the organized, institutionalized co-operation of many individuals, and for that matter also of institutions with other institutions.

That, then, which is of course a very great deal, is obviously part of what is required if amelioration of the human predicament, or perhaps merely the avoidance of its excessive deterioration, is to be practically possible; if we have the requisite information and technical skills, and if there are institutional forms for bringing about the application of knowledge and skills in directed co-operative undertakings, then many things towards human betterment *can* be done. But this of course does not ensure that they will be. That is a problem of a totally different kind.

Well, at least one idea for its solution comes readily to mind. If, as has been suggested, humans have, placed as they are, a certain inherent propensity to act to the disadvantage or detriment of other humans, and even of themselves, then, if they are not to do so, they can be *made* not to do so. If, for instance, they are prone to be a good deal less concerned with the wants, needs, and interests of others than with their own, then, if they are to act in some other or in the general interest rather than purely in their own, they can be made so to act. What is required, one may reason, for the suitable modification of the patterns of behaviour towards which people are 'naturally' prone, may thus be some suitably designed system of coercion. People must be given an interest, which they do not just naturally have, in doing things which they are not just naturally inclined towards doing; and this is exactly what a system of coercion can supply.

Now there is every reason to think that this is part of the answer; but there is also every reason to think that it is not and could not be, as perhaps Hobbes thought it was, the sole and whole answer. Part of the answer, certainly: taking things as they are and have been and are likely to continue to be, it is not deniable that there are people who are deflected from acting damagingly to others, or even to themselves, solely or mainly by the anticipation of consequences disagreeable to themselves if they so act – consequences liable to be deliberately imposed on them by others, by whom to that extent they can be said to be coerced. No doubt the most conspicuous example here is law. A community without laws is not absolutely inconceivable; and in fact rather small-scale examples actually exist. It is not inconceivable that a system of law should be non-coercive, that is, should make no provision for the actual punishment of law-breakers; and on a small and rather informal scale, in some clubs for example, something like this is sometimes actually the case. Again, the prevention or diminution by coercive means of damaging conduct is by no means, of course, the only object, not even the only avowed or ostensible object, of legal systems. But it clearly is part of the ostensible object, and probably always of the actual object too; and though some would argue that ideally such systems of coercion would be dispensable, it is pretty clear that they are in fact a practical necessity in nearly all circumstances. If society at large suddenly resolved, in the manner of what used to be regarded as progressive schools, completely to dismantle all machinery of coercion, there is plenty of reason to apprehend that things on the whole would go rather worse as a result than they actually do.

However, it is not true, and scarcely could be true, that people are brought to abstain from acting damagingly to others, or even to themselves, solely by coercion or by coercive deterrence. There is a practical point here, and also, I think, a kind of logical point. In the first place, if nothing but coercion kept people in order, then the machinery of coercion would have to be very vast – police, say, might have to equal in number the rest of the population, or at any rate somehow be ubiquitous and powerful enough for their surveillance to be pretty continuous and continuously effective. In practice this seems, in most societies, not in fact to be necessary for the purpose. (Though vast coercive systems are not unknown, it is more than doubtful whether it is for *this* purpose that they are maintained.) But it seems a point of no less importance that coercion is itself something that people do; such a system is directed and executed, after all, by people. If it is to do any good, or to do good rather than harm, then it must be directed and executed (let us say vaguely) properly; and it seems that it could not solely be coercion that brought this about. If coercion is ever to operate, except by pure chance, in any general interest, it seems reasonable to hold that there must be some persons, indeed many persons, prepared to act in that general interest without themselves being coerced into doing so. Perhaps this is not absolutely conclusive. It would be possible to argue, as perhaps one could say that Hobbes did, that there is neither necessity nor point in making the supposition that a system of coercion should be 'properly' directed or run – that is, that any system at all is so vastly better than none that its existence, however oppressive or even ferocious it might be, would still be on balance in the general interest; nor is it perhaps completely impossible that those who coerce others should, in some way if not exactly the same way, be themselves coerced. But these may well be thought not to be realistic speculations. As things are and long have been and are likely to continue to be, it is reasonable to say that the beneficent operation of any coercive system requires that there should be, at least sometimes and in some people, some propensity to act beneficently without being made to do so. Of course I am not suggesting for a moment that all coercive systems actually are beneficent.

We thus come to what seems clearly most important in the present connection. If any of those things towards the amelioration of the human predicament which can be done are to be done in fact, then not only must people sometimes be *made* to do things which they are not just naturally disposed to do anyway; they must also sometimes voluntarily, without coercion, act otherwise than people are just naturally disposed to do. It is necessary that people should acquire, and should seek to ensure that others acquire, what may be called *good dispositions* – that is, some readiness on occasion voluntarily to do desirable things which not all human beings are just naturally disposed to do anyway, and similarly not to do damaging things.

We may say, then, speaking still in quite monstrously general terms, that, if things are not actually to go quite so badly as, given the nature of the human predicament, they are inherently liable to do, there are conspicuously four sorts of general *desiderata* – knowledge, so that what is in fact amelioratively practicable is brought within the scope of feasibility by human action; organization, so that the doings of many people and of groups of people can be brought into directed, co-operative, non-conflicting channels; coercion, so that at least to some extent people may be made to behave in desirable ways, and stopped from behaving otherwise; and 'good dispositions', that is, some degree of readiness voluntarily to act desirably, and to abstain from behaving otherwise. Now it will be evident that all these are elaborately interrelated. The acquisition of knowledge is often, and nowadays increasingly, a matter for organized, co-operative, institutionalized effort; so also is its dissemination when acquired, its preservation, and its transmission in such institutions as schools and universities. The maintenance of any organization, or of co-operative behaviour within it, will sometimes call for some measures of coercion; and knowledge is needed about forms of organization themselves, how they work, to what ends and in what circumstances they are appropriate, how they may go wrong. A system of coercion, conspicuously in the highly developed and formalized shape of a system of law, must be operated in highly organized, institutionalized ways; and again a great deal needs to be known, if we are to know when and how any such system can be usefully, effectively brought to bear. But it seems to me reasonable to insist that, among all these ramified and mutually inter-acting *desiderata*, a certain absolute priority must be seen as attaching to human dispositions. We have already found, in an earlier chapter, some reason for thinking that, of the limitations which constitute (in a sense) the human predicament, the most important are those that might be called most 'internal' to human beings – that is, limitations of rationality and sympathy. It may now seem to be the case that, essentially for just the same reasons, what is crucial for betterment is the promotion of 'good dispositions'. All the other things – acquiring, disseminating, preserving, and transmitting knowledge, setting up and maintaining organizations and institutions, devising and operating means of making people do things – all of these things are things that people do: so that everything in the end depends on their readiness to do them, and to do them at least some of the time without being compelled to do so. Moreover, as Kant would have insistently and rightly pointed out, none of those other things we have mentioned is, so to speak, of itself and intrinsically beneficent. Increased knowledge increases the capacity to do harm as well as good; prodigious feats of organization may go into the successful waging of destructive and wholly maleficent wars; people may be coerced, and often are, into behaving worse than they would do if left to themselves. All these things, one might say, have to do with our capacity to influence the way things go; they do not determine how that capacity is to be used, or whether it is to be used to our or anyone's detriment or benefit. What matters most is what, of the things we can do, we choose to do; if this goes wrong, then everything goes wrong, and only more wrong, the more efficiently it goes.

There comes into view, then, among very general *desiderata* for the betterment of the human predicament, a distinction which seems to be of great and (I hope) of obvious importance – a distinction, namely, between what makes betterment possible, and what tends to bring it about that it actually occurs; roughly, between means available to people for the improvement of their lot, and the disposition to make beneficial use of those means. Moreover, if we now look again at this topic of human dispositions, it seems possible to discern here also a similar distinction – between, as one may put it, those dispositions whose tendency is to increase the effectiveness, or capacity, of a person, and those which tend to determine to what uses his capacities will be put.

The dispositions I have in mind under the first head may all be regarded, I think, as different varieties of the disposition to accept, or tolerate, or endure what, in various ways, may in itself be disagreeable. Pertinacious exertion, whether physical or mental, is often – not always – in itself somewhat disagreeable; there is some natural inclination to abandon what is found laborious; and the propensity, on appropriate occasions, not to do so, is rightly and for clear reasons regarded as a desirable disposition. The prospect or presence of danger is disagreeable; but it is very plainly desirable that a person should not always indulge his natural inclination to escape or avoid it. Somewhat similarly, there is an endless range and variety of discomforts which it is both disagreeable and often necessary to incur, and an endless range and variety of satisfactions or indulgences which it is both unpleasant but often highly desirable not to pursue. And in the 'good dispositions' which consist in such readinesses to endure the disagreeable we have, as will readily be seen, a large number of generally recognized and familiar virtues – conspicuously, industriousness, courage, and self-control; but many others also.

Now as to these I offer the suggestion – which I take not to be just arbitrary, though I have also no doubt at all that it will not be universally accepted – that, while there is clear and good reason to regard these dispositions as virtues, it would not be unreasonable to hold that they are not *moral* virtues. They may be, indeed in some degree they certainly are, necessary conditions of the effective exercise of moral virtues, as indeed of effective action of any kind; but one may still wish to say that they *are* not moral virtues. Whether this suggestion is acceptable or not, let me at any rate offer forthwith my reasons for making it. It seems to me that there would be two good reasons for wishing to say this, or perhaps one reason put in two rather different ways. In the first place these virtues, while of course they are not necessarily, yet they may be exclusively and entirely, what might be called self-profiting. That is, the acquisition and exercise of these virtues is not only typically essential to, but could in principle be wholly directed to, the attainment of an agent's personal interests or ends – possibly, indeed, of ends of his to the gross damage or neglect of the interests of others. If, for instance, the dominant object of my life is to maintain, by fair means or foul, my personal power and ascendancy over some group, or party, or gang, or country, or empire, I may well display, and need to display, exceptional industry in maintaining and defending my system of despotism, great courage in resisting the pressures and machinations of my opponents and enemies, and marked self-control in adhering, perhaps sometimes in the teeth of great temptation and difficulty, to the sagacious promotion of my long-run interests, undistracted by impulse, self-indulgence, passion, or pleasure. Courage, asceticism, iron self-control, resolution in the face of hardship or danger or difficulty – these are almost standard equipment for the really major destroyers, whether military, political, or criminal, or all three at once. Thus, while the dispositions here in question are undoubted virtues, they are virtues all of which a very bad man might have; and while probably such qualities are admirable even in a bad man, he is not, it seems to me quite reasonable to maintain, *morally* the better for his possession of those admirable qualities.

Second, while these dispositions certainly do tend to counter-vail, as it were, something in the human predicament which contributes importantly to its natural tendency to turn out rather badly, they do not tend quite directly to countervail that in the predicament which there seems reason to regard, both in fact and moral theory, as really central. For these dispositions tend to countervail, and are genuinely admirable in so far as they do so, what might be called natural human *weaknesses* – varieties, that is, of the natural inclination to evade or avoid, in its various forms, the burdensome or disagreeable. But they have in themselves no tendency at all to counteract the limitation of human sympathies; and this is really just another way of saying that, as I mentioned a moment ago, they may be wholly self-profiting, and even very damaging to others than the agent himself.

This, then, invites the suggestion, which I am perfectly ready to make, that the paradigmatic *moral* virtues may be, not these, but rather those good dispositions whose tendency is directly to countervail the limitation of human sympathies, and whose exercise accordingly is essentially – though indeed not, by itself, necessarily effectively – good *for* persons other than the agent himself. Let us see what profit we can extract from this proposition.

What questions are they, then, that can appropriately be put to the hypothesis that we now have in view? We are operating with the idea that, 'good dispositions' being crucially important to abatement of the ills inherent in the human predicament, one might with reason regard as specifically *moral virtues* those which, not being essentially, or even potentially, exclusively self-profiting, would tend to countervail those particular ills liability to which is to be laid at the door of the limitedness of human sympathies. So, if we seek further light on what these good dispositions would be, we need now to consider in a little more detail what those particular ills are – that is, in what ways, in consequence of the limitedness of human sympathies, people are typically *liable* to act so as to worsen, or not to act so as to ameliorate, the predicament.

The first step on this path, at any rate, seems an easy one to take. If I am exclusively, or even predominantly, concerned with the satisfaction of my own wants, interests, or needs, or of those of some limited group such as my family, or friends, or tribe, or country, or class, with whose interests and ends I am naturally disposed to sympathize, then I, other members of that group, or the group as a whole, may be naturally prone to act directly to the detriment of other persons, non-members of the group, or of other groups. I may be inclined, from competitiveness or mere indifference or even active malevolence, to do positive harm to others, whether in the form of actual injury to them, or of frustration and obstruction of the satisfaction of their wants, interests, and needs. There is here, that is to say, a liability to act simply *maleficently* – harmfully, damagingly – to others, quite directly, either out of sheer unconcern with the damage so inflicted, or even out of a positive taste for the infliction of damage on persons or groups outside the circle of one's sympathies. That being so, it can scarcely seem controversial to say that *one* of the 'good dispositions' we are in search of will be the disposition to abstain from (deliberate, unjustified) maleficence. Of course, if we nominate this disposition as one of the moral virtues, it may reasonably be remarked that it is not, in a sense, very much of a virtue; a disposition, that is to say, not to act deliberately maleficently towards other persons, from sheer unconcern for or active malevolence towards them, is, one may hopefully suppose, just normally to be expected in normal persons, who accordingly come up for commendation on this account only if their non-maleficence is exceptional in degree, or maintained in the face of exceptional temptation, or provocation, or difficulty. However, the propensity *not* to act injuriously towards others whenever one has, or might have, some 'natural' inclination to do so, while perhaps not specially creditable in ordinary circumstances, is still very clearly of fundamental importance; for it is obvious what a gangster's world we should find ourselves in without it – and indeed do find ourselves in, when and so far as this disposition is absent.

The next step seems also, in general terms, scarcely more problematic. If we need, and if humans in general do not just naturally, regularly, and reliably have, the disposition of non-maleficence, just the same can plainly be said of the disposition towards positive beneficence. The limitedness of sympathies tends often to make it not just natural to interest oneself directly in another's good; there is need, then, for cultivation of the disposition to do so, which will very often take the particular form of readiness to give *help* to others in their activities. It seems reasonable to hold, and indeed practically impossible not to hold, that responsibility for pursuit of an individual's good is primarily his own – partly for the reason that it is primarily for him to say (though of course he cannot say infallibly) what that good is, and partly for the plain, practical reason that, in normal circumstances, if everyone embroils himself persistently, however well-meaningly, in other people's concerns rather than his own, a considerable measure of chaos and cross-purposes is likely to ensue. There are, however, many ends a person may have which cannot be secured by his own efforts alone. There are common ends, to be secured only by the co-operation of many. There are some persons who have particular claims upon the beneficence of particular other persons. And there are some persons who, though perhaps without any special claims, should be helped because their need of help is exceptionally great, or their ability to help themselves exceptionally restricted. Not much more than this could be said in quite general terms. People and societies clearly differ a good deal, for a variety of reasons, in their assessment of the proportion of time, talents, efforts, and resources that an individual should devote to ends and interests other than his own; moreover, what is required in this way, what there is scope for, depends very much on the organization and institutions of particular societies. How far, for instance, there is need and room for private charity will depend on the extent to which public provision is made for the relief of indigence. But it is worth remarking, I think, that disagreement on this issue is often disagreement on the facts, at least in part. It was once held, notoriously, that it is *in fact* most advantageous for everybody that each, by and large, should pursue and promote his own interests single-mindedly; and though this thesis no doubt was often disingenuously asserted by those who fancied their chances in the envisaged free-for-all, and indeed is certainly not true without qualification, it is still, I suppose, a question of fact, and an unsettled question, in what ways and to what extent it needs to be qualified. In any case we are not attempting to settle here exactly what, in one case or another, the proper exercise of this virtue would actually consist in; what here matters, and what in general terms seems scarcely disputable, is that, along with non-maleficence, it *is* a virtue.

What else? Well, so far we have laid at the door of 'limited sympathies', and accordingly have affirmed the need to countervail, the inclination to act damagingly to others towards whom one is not 'naturally' sympathetic, and not to act beneficently when such action is needed or claimed. I believe that we should now add, as an independent requirement, the disposition not to *discriminate*, as surely most humans have some natural propensity to do, to the disadvantage of those outside the limited circle of one's natural concern. If, for instance, twenty people have a claim upon, or are substantially in need of, some service or benefit that I can provide, it seems not enough merely to say that I should not refuse it; it must be added that I should not help or benefit some of them *less* merely because, for instance, I may happen to like them less, or be less well-disposed towards them. The general name for this good disposition is, I take it, fairness. Of course it is commonly supposed, and indeed it would be unrealistically inhuman not to suppose, that actual sympathies and natural ties quite often justify discriminatory treatment; nevertheless, it must be observed that these should issue in discriminatory treatment only when, as is not always the case, they do actually justify it. Once again it would be inappropriate and probably quite unprofitable to try here to specify in any detail what, in this case or that, the exercise of this good disposition would actually consist in; what matters here is merely the very general proposition that, as an essential corrective to the arbitrariness and inequality and deprivation liable otherwise to result from the haphazard incidence of limited sympathies, it surely *is* a 'good disposition' to be ready, on appropriate occasions, to recognize the need for or claims to good, or to relief from ill, of those in whose good or ill one may have no natural concern whatever. And we may add that the importance of this virtue of fairness tends, evidently but interestingly, to increase with the increase of scope and occasions for its exercise. For very many people, after all, their power to help or harm others is actually so limited as probably to be confined, on most occasions, to persons who may well be within the circle of their natural concern; but as such power increases, it is increasingly likely to expand its scope over persons to whom one may personally be wholly indifferent, or even of whom one may know nothing at all. This is to say, surely truly, that the virtue of fairness – or, more formally, justice – is a more important virtue in, for instance, political rulers, judicial functionaries, commanders of armies, heads of institutions, and so on, than it is in the case of relatively obscure private persons, whose circumstances may confront them with relatively little occasion to exercise it.

Then one more thing. If we consider the situation of a person, somewhat prone by nature to an exclusive concern with his own, or with some limited range of, interests and needs and wants, living among other persons more or less similarly constituted, we see that there is one device in particular, very often remarkably easy to employ, by which he may be naturally more or less inclined to, so to speak, carve out his egoistical way to his own, and if necessary at the expense of other, ends; and that is *deception*. It is possible for a person, and often very easy, by doing things, and especially in the form of saying things, to lead other persons to the belief that this or that is the case; and one of the simplest and most seductive ways of manipulating and manœuvring other persons for the sake of one's own ends is that of thus operating self-interestedly upon their beliefs. Clearly this is not, necessarily, directly damaging. We all hold from time to time an immense range and variety of false beliefs, and very often are none the worse for doing so; we are the worse for it only if, as is often not the case, our false belief leads or partly leads us actually to act to our detriment in some way. Thus, I do not necessarily do you any harm at all if, by deed or word, I induce you to believe what is not in fact the case; I may even do you good, possibly by way, for example, of consolation or flattery. Nevertheless, though deception is thus not necessarily directly damaging, it is easy to see how crucially important it is that the natural inclination to have recourse to it should be counteracted. It is, one might say, not the implanting of false beliefs that is damaging, but rather the generation of the suspicion that they may be being implanted. For this undermines trust; and, to the extent that trust is undermined, all co-operative undertakings, in which what one person can do or has reason to do is dependent on what others have done, are doing, or are going to do, must tend to break down. I cannot reasonably be expected to go over the edge of a cliff on a rope, for however vital an object, if I cannot trust you to keep hold of the other end of it; there is no sense in my asking you for your opinion on some point, if I do not suppose that your answer will actually express your opinion. (Verbal communication is doubtless the most important of all our co-operative undertakings.) The crucial difficulty is precisely, I think, that deception is so easy. Deliberately saying, for instance, what I do not believe to be true is just as easy as saying what I do believe to be true, and may not be discriminable from it by even the most practised and expert of observers; thus, uncertainty as to the credentials of *any* of my performances in this respect is inherently liable to infect *all* my performances – there are, so to speak, no 'natural signs', or there may be none, by which the untrustworthy can be distinguished from the veracious, so that, if any may be deceptive, all may be. Nor, obviously, would it be any use merely to devise some special formula for the purpose of explicitly signalling non-deceptive performance; for, if the performance may be deceptive, so also might be the employment of any such formula – it is easy to say 'I really mean it', not really meaning it, and hence to say 'I really mean it' without thereby securing belief. Even *looking* sincere and ingenuous, though perhaps slightly more difficult than simply saying that one is, is an art that can be learned. In practice, of course, though there may be very few persons indeed whom we take to be non-deceptive on all occasions, we do manage, and rightly, to trust quite a lot of the people quite a lot of the time; but this depends on the supposition that, while sometimes they may have special reasons, which with luck and experience and judgement we may come to understand, for resorting to deceptive performance on some occasions, they do not do so simply *whenever* it suits their book. If one could not make even this milder supposition, then co-operative involvement among persons would become, if not impossible, at any rate more or less useless and unreasonable – like political agreements between bourgeois politicians and Marxists.

Parenthetically, I should like to mention here, though not to discuss, the curious case, which does also occur, of persons who, while seldom or perhaps even never deliberately speaking or acting, to suit their book, contrary to their real beliefs, seem to have the knack of so tailoring their beliefs as to suit their book. This singular propensity is, in a way, even more damaging than that of the common-or-garden liar; it is compatible, for one thing, with extreme self-righteousness; but, more importantly, while the liar for his own ends misrepresents the way things are, he may perfectly retain the capacity to realize how they are, and may thus be thought to be, in a sense, more redeemable than one whose capacity to see straight is itself corrupted. But we impinge here on self-deception, a complex topic.

We suggest, then, that, in the general context of the human predicament, there are these four (at least) distinguishable damaging, or non-ameliorative, types of propensity which tend naturally to emanate directly from 'limited sympathies' – those of maleficence, non-beneficence, unfairness, and deception. If now we apply the supposition that the 'object' of morality is to make the predicament less grim than, in a quasi-Hobbesian state of nature, it seems inherently liable to be, and to do so specifically by seeking to countervail the deleterious liabilities inherent in 'limited sympathies', we seem to be led to four (at least) general types of good disposition as those needed to countervail the above-mentioned four types of propensity; and these dispositions will be, somewhat crudely named, those of non-maleficence, fairness, beneficence, and non-deception. We venture the hypothesis that these (at least) are fundamental *moral virtues*.

But we can now manipulate this conclusion a little. If it were agreed that we have here, in these 'good dispositions', four moral virtues, it could scarcely be contentious to derive from this the proposition that we have here, by the same token, four fundamental moral *standards*, or moral *principles*. To have and to display, say, the moral virtue of non-deception could be said to be to regulate one's conduct in conformity to a *principle* of non-deception, or to refer to that as to a *standard* in one's practical decisions. But such a principle would be a principle of judgement as well as of decision. That is, if I accept a principle of non-deception, I may judge others to be morally condemnable in so far as (without excuse) their acts constitute breaches of it, or morally praiseworthy in so far as they (laudably) comply with it in practice. And thus we can say what a 'moral reason' is. Namely, it is a consideration, about some person, or some person's character, or some specimen of actual or possible conduct, which tends to establish in the subject concerned conformity or conflict with a moral principle. That your act would inflict wanton damage on some other person would be a 'moral reason' for judging that – at least 'from the moral point of view' – you ought not so to act, since it tends to establish that your act would be in conflict with the moral principle of non-maleficence, or, to put just the same point in a different way, would be inconsistent with exercise of the moral virtue of non-maleficence. Moral 'pros and cons' – an expression that cropped up in an earlier chapter – will be those considerations, perhaps very complex and very numerous, concerning some particular case that comes up for judgement, which indicate respectively conformity to or conflict with some one or more moral principles.

I will end this chapter by offering two observations which, while both comparatively obvious, are of some importance. First, it seems to me that the 'principles' we have sketchily elicited, and as to which we offer the hypothesis that they are basic *moral* principles, have to be accepted as independent principles, not reducible either to one another or to anything else. There is indeed, if I am right, some bond of union between them, as well as a very manifest *rationale* behind them – something, that is, that makes it possible coherently to explain why it is that they are grouped together as *moral* principles, and why compliance with them should constitute moral *virtue*; the suggestion is, namely, that they are alike in the respect that their voluntary recognition would tend to counteract the maleficent liabilities of limited sympathies, and in *that* way to work towards amelioration of the human predicament. However, though alike in this, they remain independent. For there is not *one* way in which beings of limited sympathies are inherently liable to act to each other's detriment, but *several* ways, and thus several independent 'good dispositions' to be desiderated. This emerges, I think, reasonably clearly from what has been said. It would be just possible, I suppose, though extremely artificial, to class non-maleficence as a sub-species of beneficence; but it seems to me both more natural and more explicit to regard the principle of abstaining from avoidable and unjustified damage as *different* from that of doing solicited or unsolicited good. Abstaining from theft is not a special kind of philanthropy. Fairness, again, is a *different* requirement from that of non-maleficence, or of beneficence; it may often be the case that a maleficent act is unfair, but that is to say about it two things, not one thing; and even if, as may not always be the case, some act of fairness is also an act of beneficence, still the reason for judging it to be the first will not be the same as that for judging it to be the second. An act of deception, as we said before, is not necessarily maleficent; and again, if I benefit you in acting non-deceptively, to show that I do benefit you is a quite different matter from showing that I do not deceive you – even when these go together, they are not the same. To tell you the truth to the best of my ability is not at all the same thing as to tell you what I judge it would be of benefit to you to be told. It has been held that deception is always a breach of the principle of

G

justice, but this again seems to me, though just possible, un-desirably artificial; deception, I would think, is appropriately classed as unjust only if the victim has some sort of *special* claim, not merely that which any person has on any other person what-ever, not to be deceived. It is perhaps specifically unfair for me to lie to you when you have trustingly favoured me with your confidence; but it is not in the same way *unfair* of me to deceive a total stranger.

There are two major reasons, I believe, why recognition of this fact of independence is of considerable importance. The first is theoretical. Philosophers, professionally in pursuit of systematic unity, and feeling (rightly in my view) that behind morality there is to be discerned an – in some sense – single *rationale*, seem often to have been taken with the idea that perhaps there is really just *one* fundamental moral principle. This seems to be an error. It may be that there is one, very general, end in view; but there is not, as one might put it, just one means to that end. And the second point is practical, or anyway less purely theoretical; it is that what I take to be the plurality and independence of moral principles implies that 'moral reasons' may conflict. We are in-veterately liable in any case to be perplexed in practice by con-flicting considerations; even if, for instance, we are charged with the single requirement of selecting for an appointment the best instructor in philosophy, the circumstance of some applicant's exceptional philosophical ability may conflict with his obvious lack of interest in teaching, or inability to express himself com-prehensibly to the student mind. Or again, an arbitrator's deci-sion that would do justice to the claims of one party may some-times, by exactly the same standard, imply injustice to the claims of another. But if, in morality, there are anyway independent principles, there is the obvious possibility that what conformity with one would require would involve conflict with another; there may, that is, be clear moral pros *and* cons in the very same case; and if that is so, it seems to me quite impossible to exclude the possibility that predicaments may arise which are, literally, morally insoluble. One would indeed wish to avoid this conclusion if possible, but I do not myself see how this possibility of genu-ine insolubility is to be excluded. It is clear that moral principles *may* point in opposite directions; and I can discern no ground on which one could pronounce *in general* which, in such a case, is to predominate over another. This may indeed be possible in special cases. One may have, as a judge perhaps, a *special* commitment to justice, as a scholar to truth, or as a friend to beneficence. But still, if there is independence, there may be conflict; and if there may be conflict, there may be irresoluble perplexity. I do not know, however, that one need be particularly appalled by this conclusion; for even if there exists the possibility of irresoluble perplexity, I know of no reason for supposing, in the Existentialist manner, that irresoluble perplexity is *typical* of moral decision, or that the typical terminal process in morals is that of arbitrary choice. And one may add that even if, like the simple Utilitarian, one held that there was only one moral principle really, it would still have to be admitted that cases might arise in which considerations, weighed by that one principle alone, might point, with exactly equal force, in opposite directions. Thus reduction to a single principle, even if it were possible, would not wholly get us out of this difficulty, so far as it is one.

My second comment is this. It is obvious but important that morality, seen from the angle that we have here adopted, does not offer an answer to the question 'how one should live', in at any rate some important senses of that queer, obscure phrase. But here there are obscurities that call for a little untangling.

What is one to make, anyway, of the question 'how one should live', given honourable mention by Plato and by many of his successors? It may look, from one angle at least, a pretty senseless question. Where we have some reasonably well-defined, determinate task or performance, it makes clear sense to ask how that task or performance should be done; one understands the question how one should set about catching trout, reducing consumer demand, seeking an interview with the Prime Minister, or trying perhaps to become Prime Minister oneself. But what is 'living'? Presumably it consists in doing things, doing anything whatever, in thinking this or that, having dreams and feelings and moods of some sort, and so on; and what sense does it make to enquire how *that* should be done? In this sense, the question how one ought to live looks in no better case than the question how one ought to cook – not how one ought to cook carrots, or cabbage, or kippers, or anything in particular, but *simply* how one ought to *cook*. A senseless question, one is tempted to say, has no sensible answer.

Presumably, however, there are other ways in which the words can be taken, in which they can be seen to pose a decently intelligible question, though not, indeed, always a question that has a reasonable answer. First, the question 'how one should live' might be taken to mean: what goals should one seek to achieve in the course of one's life? Two comments on this. First, while this is, I think, a decently intelligible question, there seems to me every reason to suppose that there is not, quite in general, any sensible answer to it. For is there any goal in life at all of which one could say, quite in general, that 'one' – that is, anyone and everyone – should aim at achieving it? The goals, I suppose, that there is reason, at any rate *ceteris paribus*, for me to try to achieve are those that I might be expected to find satisfactory, if I should achieve them. But what those would be, is a function of what sort of person I am, am capable of becoming, or likely to become; and not everyone, both obviously and fortunately, is the same sort of person. The goals appropriate to a 'man of action' are not, surely, to be recommended to the contemplative scholar, the dedicated artist, the religious recluse. Such people will pursue, and properly pursue, quite different goals; there is no way in which, in that sense, they *all* should live.

Second, it is clear that 'morality', as here envisaged, does not pronounce, in this sense of the question, on how one ought to live – fortunately, indeed, for morality, if I am right in suggesting that the question so taken is not one that can be reasonably answered anyway. For morality, as I see it, does not as such set definite goals before us, or nominate specific ends as those at which we should aim; it should rather be seen, I suggest, as propounding principles to which by and large our conduct should conform in the pursuit of our ends, *whatever* those ends may be. Morality, so to speak, does not tell me whether to be a musician, a manufacturer, a professional golfer, or a hermit; it is closer to the truth to regard it as setting certain limits on what, as musician or manufacturer, golfer or whatever it may be, I may allowably do in the pursuit of my adopted career. We should qualify this a little. First, it may be that there are – it is obviously possible that there should be – certain ends which it would be morally condemnable to pursue at all, and which accordingly are not, from the moral point of view, to be allowably pursued within limits; it may be that morality itself excludes in this way the ends of world dictatorship, of becoming a supreme authority on bacteriological warfare, or achieving the really perfect murder, and so on. But though some may be thus excluded altogether, there remains a vast diversity, one may think, of permissible options. Second, it may obviously be that, in special circumstances, one may feel that some end is morally, so to speak, forced upon one. If I am, say, the proprietor of some industrial enterprise on which the community I live in is economically wholly dependent, and which is certain to be wound up if I do not keep it going, I may feel myself morally committed to the life of an industrialist; it might in these circumstances be morally wrong for me, though of course it is not for people in general, to adopt music or cricket as a profession, or whatever it might be. But most people, I take it, are not thus morally committed – certainly they are not thus committed by morality *itself* – to a particular form of life, to the pursuit of quite determinate goals. It seems obvious in general that people who recognize exactly the same moral principles, and who conform with them equally satisfactorily in all that they do, may nevertheless actually be doing quite different things, living quite different sorts of lives, pursuing widely different ends. There is no one way, in *that* sense, in which morality requires one to live.

But one may take 'how one ought to live' in a rather different way again. Perhaps what one is to aim at can be regarded, like Aristotle's *eudaimonia*, not so much as a goal to be achieved at some stage of one's life, but rather as a predominant *character* to be realized in one's life as a whole. But here again the two comments just made seem once more appropriate. Is there any real reason to suppose that, for everyone, there is any one general character that his life should have? Are there not, as they say, 'life-styles' of many different varieties, each in its own way appropriate to certain sorts of people? And again, does morality as such require a particular 'life-style'? There seems no reason to think so. Compliance, once again, with what morality requires seems, while no doubt not compatible with some kinds of life, yet compatible with lives of many very different kinds. There is, it may be, a particular kind of life whose outstanding character is that of concern with the requirements of morality itself – in which living a *moral* life is the predominant concern of living. But it is not at all clear to me that one must suppose that morality itself requires that this should be so. One might think that to be *predominantly* concerned in one's life with, above all else, exact fulfilment of the requirements of morality is to exhibit a kind of moral extremism, or fanaticism, which it is not morally required of everyone that they should do.

Of course, if 'how should one live?' means 'in conformity with what principles?', then morality as we envisage it does offer an answer; for, precisely, it proposes principles for us to live by. But it does not, I think, even in this sense, offer a *complete* answer; for there are, of course, principles of conduct, of many different sorts, which are not *moral* principles, to which nevertheless it is proper that attention should be paid in considering by what principles one's life ought to be lived.

I can sum up, I think, what I am suggesting here by saying that, so far as I can see, the topic of morality is not at all the same as that of what used to be called 'the Good Life'. I doubt, for reasons indicated, whether the latter venerable topic is really a very useful one to discuss; for, since it is evident that there are people of very different kinds, with widely different tastes and talents, inclinations and abilities, it seems only reasonable to suppose that there are many *different* ways in which human lives may be satisfactorily, successfully, and admirably lived. But in any case morality, in my view, is only part of this topic. Morality, with the end of ameliorating the human predicament, essentially prescribes what might be called conditions *within which* lives are to be lived and ends to be pursued; but many different lives can be accommodated within those conditions; and for the 'good life' – *any* good life – much more is required than simply that those limiting conditions should not be transgressed. One might live, come to that, a very poor life indeed – unsuccessful, unhappy, incoherent, frustrated, unproductive – without necessarily going *morally* astray at any point at all. The possession and exercise of moral virtues may be its own reward; but it is by no means the *only* reward that a reasonable man would hope for.

.   .   .

I want now to cast back a little, in order to take note of and, I hope, in the next chapter, to deal with, an objection of some importance. Towards the end of the foregoing chapter, in rejecting the idea that the exercise of moral judgement essentially consists in the application of *rules*, I wrote that in the exercise of such judgement there should rather occur 'the constantly repeated attempt to achieve the best judgement on the full, concrete merits of each individual case. One should thus consider what there is reason to do or not do, or what view there is reason to take, rather than, less discriminatingly, what is required by some rule, or permitted or ruled out by some rule.' We are now in a position to put a little more substance into these words, in the light of what we have been saying about 'moral reasons'. A moral reason, we have said, is a consideration about some subject tending to establish conformity or conflict with a moral principle; and we have ventured some suggestions as to what the very general, fundamental moral principles might be. On this basis, we can say that the exercise of *moral* judgement involves the taking notice, and due weighing, of all pertinent moral *reasons* – of the *moral* pros and cons (of which both, very probably, will be present) as determined in the case in question by moral principles. Now it may, I believe, be thought with some plausibility that to offer such an account of the exercise of moral judgement (admittedly a mere skeleton) is to leave the picture importantly incomplete. For what, it may be said, about *obligation*? It may be that, in merely considering what, from the moral point of view, one ought or ought not to do, one has merely to consider what – 'on the full, concrete merits of each individual case' – there is moral reason, or a balance of moral reasons, for doing or not doing. But what if one has an *obligation* to act in some determinate, particular way? What if one is, not merely morally justified in acting in a certain way by a balance of moral reasons, but morally *bound* so to act? Is it not, one may think, part of what it *is* to be thus 'bound' that one is *not* to consider the pros and cons of the particular case? To assess the force of these questions, we had better consider in some detail the phenomenon of obligation, and whether it requires what we have said hitherto to be amended.

7. Obligations

Some philosophers have not, it seems, recognized any distinction at all between what, morally speaking, one ought to do, and what one has an obligation to do. In their view, apparently, to say that one has an obligation to do something is merely another way of saying that one ought to do it, or that that would be the right thing for one to do, and vice-versa. But this seems clearly wrong. As I drive up to London in my comfortable car, you may feel and may tell me that (out of beneficence) I ought to stop and give a lift to the inoffensive-looking person standing hopefully, thumb suitably protruded, at the side of the road; and I might agree with that; but I would not, I think, agree that I have, or am under, an *obligation* to do so. I am not, we assume, plying for hire or in the public service, so that I have not in that way an obligation to supply transportation to those who ask for it; nor am I, we assume, the only car-driver on the road, the sole means by which this person can ever get to London at all. No doubt I do have some obligations towards him; for instance, as the person in charge of a motor vehicle, I have an obligation, indeed a duty, not to drive it in a manner that would put him in danger. That much, merely as a driver, I am bound to do; but I am not *bound*, as the driver of a private car, to offer lifts to everyone, or even to anyone, who may solicit that service, even though it may be that as a matter of fact I ought to do so in some cases. There is a distinction between those things that I am bound to do, and those that merely, for certain reasons, I ought to do. I do not, in sometimes failing to do what I ought to do, necessarily therein default on my obligations.

(It may be remarked by the way that failure to make any distinction between one's obligations and what one ought to do has been, in my opinion, a considerable nuisance in moral philosophy. For it has led some theorists to assimilate all 'oughts' to obligations, others to attenuate all obligations to 'oughts', and thus to generate, out of what should be compatible elements of a single doctrine, the appearance of irreconcilably conflicting schools of thought. Here, as elsewhere in philosophy, much controversy has been carried on between persons who, having a firm hold of some part of the truth, insist that the part they have hold of is really the whole.)

Now, in this notion of being morally *bound*, there are, it seems to me, at least two distinguishable elements, one of which need cause us no particular trouble or perplexity. Sometimes, I think, one may say that one has an obligation to act in a certain way, having in mind in so saying merely that one finds reasons of exceptionally conclusive force and clarity why one ought so to act. Rather similarly, in such a case, instead of saying merely 'I ought to', one may express one's sense of the clear, compulsive force of the reasons why one ought to, by saying 'I must'. I may thus feel that I *must*, say, continue to look after the interests of my aged, petulant, and rather helpless employer, even though I am not formally bound to him in any way, and might be widely regarded as quite justified, in view of the perhaps less than generous terms of my employment, in taking my services elsewhere. I may thus feel an obligation to the feckless but friendly natives of my colonial territory, even though I am formally quite entitled to retire with honour and think no more about them. It is significant, I think, that one finds it natural to say that one may *feel* thus. For that way of speaking suggests, I believe not misleadingly, that it is perhaps not so much that, in this sort of case, one *is* bound, as that one *feels* so; one *feels* that one must, though one may know quite clearly that it is not really the case, in any tangible sense, that one must. What we have here, one might say, is the *sense* of having no option – of there being only one course that one can bring oneself to take, or even seriously to consider taking. Where one finds the reasons why one ought to act in a certain way to be peculiarly clear, cogent, and inescapable, it is this feeling that no other course is really – though it may be formally – open that is expressed in saying that one *must*, that one is or feels bound, that one has or feels an obligation. However, though of course in a way this is a special sort of case – there are doubtless many things one recognizes that one ought to do, without thus feeling that one *must* do them – yet this sort of case seems to introduce no novelty or difficulty of principle. This one sort of obligation – the sort that, typically, one 'feels' – is clearly continuous and *in pari materia* with those things in general of which one thinks that, for certain reasons, one ought to do them; it is only that, in these cases, the reasons seem especially clear, strong, and decisive. We seem not to be confronted then, here at any rate, with any phenomenon quite different from that of considering and concluding, on the merits of the particular case, what one ought to do; what we have said of moral reasons seems adequate to take care of this.

The case, however, that may seem to be radically different from this is that in which one not merely feels, but really has, an obligation – in which one not merely feels, psychologically or subjectively, bound to act in a certain way, but in which, in some sense or other, one really is bound. The question is whether, to accommodate this phenomenon, we have to bring in something quite different from the appraisal of reasons, some notion quite different from that of 'the merits of the case', something quite other, perhaps, than the basic principles that we seemed to be led to in the preceding chapter. What is it to be *bound*, then, and how is one's sometimes being so to be explained? I shall consider this primarily in the palmary instance of *promising*; for this is not only, it seems, an undyingly popular topic among moral philosophers, but is perhaps also the clearest and most familiar instance of being – namely, in virtue of putting oneself – under an obligation, of being bound to act, through having bound oneself, in a determinate manner. I shall suggest furthermore, in due course, that other species of obligations are to be elucidated, essentially, in just the same way as that of promises, so that we have here a good leading case, as well as a familiar one.[1]

Let us begin by considering what promises are for, or what the point typically is of the performance of promising. This is not

[1] I have profited considerably on this topic from a paper, as yet unpublished I believe, by D. W. Stampe, though I cannot be confident that he would be satisfied with my conclusions.

very mysterious. Suppose that you, living in the house next door to mine, are going to be away at the seaside for a couple of weeks, during which time your house will be uninhabited except by your cat, whose well-being is of considerable concern to you. The cat, you realize, will need food and drink while you are away; and you want somehow to make sure that food and drink will be duly provided. Well, it occurs to you that I, your neighbour, could fairly easily attend to the cat's needs for a couple of weeks; so you call in, with the necessary tins, tin-opener, and so on, and ask me to feed your cat, and I say that I will. Now that might, of course, be good enough on its own; you might feel that, since I have said that I will feed your cat, you can now go away with entirely adequate assurance that your cat will be fed. But possibly not; if you are rather exceptionally anxious about your cat, or if you suspect that, from forgetfulness or mere casualness, I am liable not always to do what I have said I will, you may seek, by committing me more firmly, to strengthen your assurance of your cat's well-being. 'Do you *promise*?', you may say. It is perhaps not quite clear, without a more detailed narrative, whether in saying this you are inviting me to take a further step – to *promise* to feed your cat, as, in merely saying that I will, I have not yet done – or whether you are just asking me to make fully explicit that my saying that I will had, and has, the force of a *promise*. But in any case the upshot is going to be the same; the point of my explicit promise, assuming that you extract one, is to strengthen your assurance that what you are asking me to do will actually be done. And this is, in general, what promises are typically for; the idea is to enable people, those to whom promises are made, to depend, or count, on other persons, the promise-makers, to do some specified thing which the promisees need or want done.

It is clear enough, of course, this being so, that there can be promises which ought not to be asked for, and ought not to be made. For one thing, since, as we have seen, to ask for a promise is normally to imply that one is not satisfied, not fully assured, by someone's merely saying that he will, to ask for a promise may sometimes be rather offensive, even insulting – it more than hints at an ascription of casualness, forgetfulness, unreliability. But clearly also you ought not, *prima facie* at any rate, to try to commit me, for some purpose of your own, to doing something that it would be unreasonably costly or difficult or disagreeable for me to do – nor, of course, to doing something which, on independent grounds, I ought not to do anyway: if I ought not to steal the Ministry's blue-prints, you ought not even to ask me to promise to steal them. Correlatively, if there is something that I ought not to do, I clearly should not promise to do it; nor should I, merely prudentially, thus commit myself to doing what I should find unreasonably burdensome, or risky, and so on. Differently, I clearly should not promise to do what I am not reasonably confident of being able to do; probably I should not promise to do what I believe the promise-seeker will find, even if he thinks otherwise, to his disadvantage; and sometimes – if, for instance, the future is very uncertain, and I cannot tell at all what my reasonable options at the relevant time are going to be – I probably ought not, by promising, to bind my hands in advance at all. I should remain uncommitted.

But how, we must clearly ask, does this *work*? Having agreed that the point of A's promising B to do X is typically to strengthen B's assurance that X will actually be done by A, we have to ask how the performance – the promise – can actually have that effect. What is it *in* the performance, or in the transaction, in virtue of which B's assurance may actually be increased? That is: what reason does B thus acquire for 'counting on' A?

Well, the first step here seems easy – though it leads immediately to a further question. Obviously, your assurance that I will actually feed your cat, your readiness to depend on my doing so if I have promised to do so, must rest on the idea that I myself will feel pretty strongly that, having promised to feed your cat, I ought actually to do so, and that, since I quite easily can, I consequently will. If I have said merely that I will, you may perhaps suspect that, in the days to come, I may come to think that I I needn't really bother, and your cat will go unfed; but if you get me to *promise*, then surely I will feel strongly that I ought to perform, and will do so accordingly. This is confirmed by the point that, if you regard me as a pretty unscrupulous and irresponsible character, quite capable of laughing off and neglecting even my promises, then you will not think it worth your while to get me to promise, or feel at all reassured if I do. That is: the assurance-creating function of a promise operates by way of inducing, in the promise-giver, a, so to speak, *extra* sense that he ought to do the thing specified in the promise, and *thus* (in the case of decently scrupulous persons) stronger reason for the promisee to anticipate that it will actually be done.

But here, of course, we have immediately a further question; namely, why (or how) does a promise induce, in the promise-giver, an 'extra' sense that he ought to do the thing specified in the promise? How does *that* work? What is in promising, what could it be, that mysteriously generates a special sort of commitment to acting in a specified way?

Now there is a certain temptation to go off here in what I think can be seen to be really the wrong direction. If we consider again what it is that a promise does, one's eye may be caught, very properly, by the circumstance that a promise typically generates an *expectation*. If A promises B to do X, then, if all goes well, B typically comes to expect that A will do X – realizing, of course, that it is actually A's intention that he should come to expect this, and that A, in promising, intended B to recognize this intention of A's. Furthermore, if the case is an ordinary case of reasonable promising, it will be appreciated by A that X is something that B wants done for some reason, quite probably for a reason well-known and quite obvious to A; we can say, that is, not only that B is expecting the performance of X by A, but is actually counting on it, will in some way mind or be put out if X is not done. But this surely, one may think, is an excellent reason why A ought to do X, and one, moreover, of which he cannot possibly be unaware; for it is not, one may think, at all a puzzling or mysterious idea that one ought to do – assuming, naturally, that one can – what one knows perfectly well that someone else is confidently expecting that one will do, and what he is in fact counting on, not merely expecting.

Now this is perfectly correct so far as it goes, and not irrelevant; nevertheless it does not, it seems to me, really bring us to the point. In the first place, if this were all that there is to be said, we would appear to be in a queer sort of chicken-and-egg predicament. B, as we have said, will reasonably count on A to do X, since he knows that A will feel strongly, having promised, that he ought to; but A, we now say, will feel that he ought to, because he will appreciate that B is counting on him to do X. But if this is right, how, so to speak, in the first place do we get off the ground? What if B, being a cautious fellow, does *not* feel assured that A will do X until he is shown why A will feel that he ought to? But then, if he does not yet feel that assurance, there is not yet (for anything we have said) any particular reason why A *should* feel that he ought to; and thus B, if un-assured, must remain un-assured forever. It seems, on this showing, that A's counting on B to do X would somehow have to spring into existence *before* there was any reason for it, since there could be such a reason only if it already existed. So something has gone wrong; or at least there must be more to be said.

We can see in another way that there must be something more to be said. Consider these two cases. First, I tell you, simply stating an intention in the course of conversation, that I will leave by car for Birmingham at about 10 a.m. to-morrow, thereby leading you, of course, as I realize, to expect that I will do so. Later that day, it transpires that you too will have to go to Birmingham to-morrow, and, the trains being inconvenient, you come to count on travelling with me, expecting as you do that I will leave by car at the time I stated. Hearing about this in due course, I conclude that, although I had been rather inclined to change my plans, I ought after all to drive to Birmingham to-morrow, since you, I now learn, are counting on me to do so and to take you with me. Second, suppose that I have been pretty regularly in the habit of driving to the beach about five o'clock every afternoon. Coming home from my office one day at four, not intending on this occasion to go out again, I learn that you have gone to the beach earlier in the day, confidently expecting that I would be there at about five o'clock as usual, and would thus save you the exhausting five-mile walk back again. Perhaps grumbling a little, I decide that I ought to go and fetch you. Now, in both these cases, I decide (not wholly unreasonably) that I ought to act in a certain way, for the reason that someone is counting on me so to act. In the first case, you expect that I will act in a certain way for the excellent reason that I actually said I was going to; in the second case, your expectation is merely an inference from your observation of my regular habits, but it may of course be an inference you are perfectly justified in making. So in each case we have a justified expectation, and an expectation, furthermore, that I will do something that you want or even need done – that is, you are counting or depending on my expected performance. Now it may very well be, as we have seen, that in cases of this sort I may conclude that I ought to do what I am counted on to do; in such cases there *is* a reason why I ought to do it, I will even, as they say, be 'letting you down' if I do not. But in neither case, of course, did I promise to do the thing in question; nor is my moral position, so to speak, at all the same as it would have been, if I had promised. In terms of the distinction sketched at the start of this chapter, though perhaps I ought to take you to Birmingham in my car, it could scarcely be said that I have an obligation to do so; and I have surely no obligation to turn out and fetch you back from the beach – perhaps I ought to do so, but as, one may think, a favour. Thus, that one ought to do what one is counted on to do, though surely not just irrelevant in the ordinary promising situation, is certainly not peculiar to, distinctive of that situation; nor does it bring in, so to speak, the sort of 'ought' that a promise distinctively involves. The element of obligation, so far, seems to have eluded capture.

So let us retrace our steps a little and think again. The position seems to be this. If I have made a promise to you to do something X, then – assuming of course that you regard me as decently trustworthy – you come thereby to count upon my doing X in due course. But it is not, it seems, that, having promised, I ought to do X merely because you are counting on me to do it; the real position seems to be the other way round – you are counting on me to do it, because I ought to. But *why* ought I to do it, then? Well, the answer, I think, that springs to the lips here, puzzling at first sight though it may be, is that I ought to do it just because *I said I would*. It is this answer, I believe, that we must try to understand, to make clear sense of.

To begin with, one may ask, can this answer possibly be even correct? How can it be, that is, that I can be 'bound' to act in a certain way through having said I would, when it is certain that I can say I will without being bound at all? We have seen this already. In the beach case, you expected me to turn up at the beach merely because I had been pretty regularly in the habit of doing so; but in the other case, you expected that I would drive to Birmingham because I had actually told you I was going to. Your expectation in this case was created by my own words; I must have known perfectly well that my words *would* create that expectation, and indeed have intended that they should do – so that I cannot in this case, disclaim responsibility for your coming to have that expectation, or try to make out that it has nothing to do with me. Nevertheless, though we said that in such a case I might well think that I ought to do what I said I was going to do (since you were counting on me to do it), yet we held that I was not really under an actual *obligation* to do that – it was not, after all, as if I had actually promised. Yet why was it not, if I had *said that I would*?

Well, we must here look more closely at these words 'I will'; for it seems that it is not saying 'I will' that is really crucial but, somehow or other, *how* this is said, and understood. Now one use of these words – a use which may (wrongly, as I shall argue) be thought not directly relevant to our present concern – is in the expression of straightforward predictions about the speaker's future, forecasts of what is going to happen to or become of him. I may say in this way, for instance, that I will be bald by the time I am fifty, or rich when my affluent great-uncle dies. One thinks here, typically, of future contingencies that are not, so to speak, up to me; these predicted things are just going to *happen* to me or they are not – my prediction is well-founded if there is reason to expect them to happen, and correct if in due course they do happen, wrong if they do not. I have nothing to *do*, as it were, in such cases except wait to see whether my prediction turns out to have been right or wrong.

Different, and at first sight more evidently relevant, is the use of 'I will' in the expression of an intention. Here it is a question, not merely of future events, but of my own future doings, of things that it is up to me, in my power, to do or not do, or that at any rate are reasonably believed to be thus in my power. So what exactly is the position, when I *thus* say 'I will'? What is primarily required, one may think, when I thus say 'I will', is that I should actually have the *present intention*. If it is wholly up to me whether I do X or not, or if at any rate it is reasonably believed that that is so, then, if I actually do not now intend to do X, I could be said to speak falsely if I say 'I will do X'; conversely, I perhaps need no further warrant for saying 'I will do X' than that, here and now, I actually intend to do so. I deceive you (or try to) if, having no intention of doing X, I say, in the intention-expressing way, that I will do X; my utterance is at any rate not deceptive, not mendacious, if, saying that I will do X, I intend to do it. There is in fact not much to choose here between 'I will' and 'I mean to' (indeed, if one could get away with taking 'will' here as the *present* tense of the verb 'to will', perhaps nothing to choose at all; but perhaps one should not press so dubious a linguistic point as that). But what about the future? How, that is, in this case does what I subsequently do, or not do, re-act back, so to speak, on what I formerly said?

In the case of a prediction it is, I suppose, the position that, if I say for instance that I will be bald by the time I am fifty, and when that time comes I am actually not bald, then what I formerly said is thereby wrong; I was – as it now turns out – mistaken in my prediction. Perhaps not culpably or in any way reprehensibly so – I may have been fully justified in issuing the prediction that I did; nevertheless, things have actually not gone as I said they were going to, so that what I said was incontestably wrong. But what if, having said – expressing an intention – that I will do X, I do not subsequently do it? There is the case here in which, having said that I will do X, I subsequently *try* to do X and fail; but the interesting case is that in which I do not even try. Well, there is, I dare say, a somewhat formalistic sense in which, here too, it can be held that what I said was wrong – just because, after all, I said 'I will do X', and actually did not. But, first, it plainly does not follow that I spoke in any way culpably; for the condition of non-mendacity in such a case is, as we have seen, that, when I say I will do X, I do actually intend to, and that condition may, of course, be fully satisfied in this case. Second, can it be said here that I was – as it turns out – mistaken? It does not appear to me that this could reasonably be said; for what would the mistake be that I could be supposed to have made? It is possible *perhaps* to be mistaken as to what one's intentions really are – to misidentify for instance, fail clearly to see for what it is, an intention one may be unwilling fully to acknowledge, even to oneself. But if I do not do X or even try to do it, having said that I would, I clearly need not have been thus mistaken in supposing that I really did mean to do it (or that I *could* do it); for I may well have meant to do it at the time (and been able to do it), but have *changed my mind*. In such a case, then, it surely is not that I turn out to have been, however wholly non-culpably, mistaken; I am not mistaken at all; for no *mistake* is involved in first intending to do something, then changing one's mind. It is not even quite clear that one has to admit, having not done X, that what one formerly said was in any sense 'wrong'; for exactly to the extent that one can hold, as in the previous paragraph, that in the expression of an intention there is nothing much to choose between 'I will' and 'I mean to', one can hold that what one formerly said stands unimpugned, so to speak, by X's being subsequently not done. I *did* mean to, after all, as I said; but I changed my mind.

It seems pretty clear, then, how it is that I can remain unbound by having said 'I will' in this intention-expressing style. So far as this has, as it has primarily, the force of 'I mean to', what my utterance is required to *fit*, if one may put it so, is my present intention; I speak properly, non-deceptively, without mendacity, if I really do mean to do whatever it is that I thus say I will do. And that does not, as it appears, depend upon my actually doing it; for of course a man who, at a certain time, intends to do something may subsequently, without necessarily incurring any reproach, change his mind and not do it. No doubt it is important to remember that, though he does not necessarily incur reproach, he may actually do so. He may be criticized for inconstancy or volatility, lack of resolution or perseverance – for though in general a man may 'always' just change his mind, there is no doubt something less than ideal in a propensity to do so too often. It might sometimes be held that he ought not to have formed his intention, whatever it was, in the first place; or again, as in the sort of case we have already considered, it might be held that he is not fully at liberty to change his mind since someone else is now depending on his acting as he originally intended to. But, in any case, the crucial point is that what he may incur reproach for, if he does, is not for now not doing X, having *said* that he would. He may be criticized simply for not doing what he had intended to do – whether or not he had had occasion to *say* that he intended to do it; or for disappointing the reasonable expectations of someone else – whether or not those were founded on his *saying* what his intention was. One's saying that one will do something, that one means to do it, is really in itself, in a sense, neither here nor there; the *consequences* of one's saying that may, in certain circumstances, have a bearing on the question whether one should actually do it or not, but one's simply saying it is not really, in itself, a relevant consideration. For I can change my mind; and if I do, though I do not of course do what I intended to do, there is thereby nothing really *wrong* with what I previously said, nor (necessarily) with what I now do.

But these considerations set before us a useful way, I think, though it may seem a surprising way, of looking at promising. Can we put it like this? To promise, we might say, is in effect – and, often, is in fact – to say 'I will', this being meant as, and taken as, not the mere expression of a present intention, but as an actual *truth* about my future behaviour.

Now, this, I am sure, will strike many people as just obviously wrong at first sight; and I had better take notice at once, before going any further, of two orthodox objections which are likely, I think, to spring instantly and clamorously to mind. First, it will doubtless be urged, an utterance purporting to convey 'a truth about my future behaviour' is – as indeed we have already conceded – surely a *prediction*: for what is a prediction, after all, but the propounding of (what is anyway offered as) a truth about the future? But then it is surely quite obvious that promises are *not* predictions. For we argue in support of predictions, we have or anyway should have grounds for them, evidence is required; but I do not have evidence for a promise, or offer grounds in support of it. Again, if I predict, you may respond with 'How do you know?'. ('How do you know the election will be held next October?'.) But there is obviously no place for asking me, if I promise, how I know. And so on.

But argument of this sort does not, if one keeps one's head, establish what it is meant, and orthodoxly taken, to establish. It is true that, for making a promise, I do not have evidence or grounds, as I presumably would have, for instance, for predicting

the date of an election. It is true also that, whereas my prediction
of the date of an election might well elicit the question 'How do
you know?', that question would be quite grossly out of place
as a response to a promise. But what *that* shows is that a promise
is not a prediction *of that kind*: it is not enough to show that it is
not a prediction at all, unless one adds the unobvious premise that
there is no other kind of prediction.

But how, you may ask, could there possibly be a prediction
not of that kind? How could there be a prediction for which I
do not have, and need not have, any evidence, or of which you
could not properly ask me how I know that my prediction is
correct? But now the answer to these questions is really, I submit, rather obvious. We must remember what is, so to speak,
the subject-matter of a promise; what my promises have to do
with is not just the future, like predictions in general, nor even
my own future, but precisely with my own future *actions* –
with that part of my future, as one may put it, that is up to me,
the shaping of which is or is reasonably believed to be wholly
in my power. But to say how that part, or some part of that part,
of my own future is going to be, I do not need evidence; for how
it will be is, not for me to find out, but *for me to say*. Thus, if I
say that it *will be* thus and so, I predict, but in a way that does
not require evidence for my prediction. For just the same reason,
though certainly it would be grossly strange for you to greet
such an utterance of mine with 'How do you know?', the reason
could be not that I have not predicted at all, but that there is *no
question* here how I know what prediction to make; for once again,
since we are talking about some part of my own future which is
or is reasonably believed to be wholly up to me, how it *will* be
is, simply, for me to say. The oddity, then, in saying that to make
a promise is to predict consists simply, I suggest, in the fact that
a promise is an odd kind of prediction; but even that really, I
believe, concedes too much, since, once one observes what this
class of predictions is *about*, there is no longer any reason to
think of them as odd at all. True, they are unlike what one may
naturally first think of as a prediction; but that is because of the
special nature of what they predict.

But, it will next be objected, how can one possibly say that to
promise is to offer a *truth* about one's future behaviour? For is it

not well known that promise-making utterances are *performative*, and as such have no truth-value at all? But this, for which Austin's authority is sometimes (wrongly) claimed, is a mere confusion. It is true, of course, that promise-making utterances are performative; namely, to issue such utterances (other conditions being appropriate for the purpose) *is* to make promises. But it is not true in general that performative utterances do not have truth-values; I may, in saying for instance 'That was a most interesting paper', *compliment* you, and also say something which is, in point of fact, untrue. What is true is that *sometimes*, in such a case, what is said has no truth-value – typically, where explicitly performative formulae are used, as in 'I congratulate you' or 'I promise to do it'. But this – to stick to our present concern with promising – does not imply that promise-making utterances cannot have truth-values; it is only to say that, in *one way* of making a promise, namely that which makes use of the explicitly performative 'I promise', what the promise-maker *says* cannot be said to be true or false.[1] There is nothing in this that makes it obviously wrong to say that, if I promise, as I very well may, by saying simply 'I will', this is meant (and taken) as a truth about my future behaviour. And to say 'I promise', we may add, may quite reasonably be held to be *in effect* exactly the same; for even if, in this case, what I say is not true or false, I *convey*, do I not, that I *will* do whatever it may be? To do this, I am inclined to say, is what promising *is*. It does not matter greatly, perhaps, if we are talking about *promising* – though it might be of great interest if we were talking about language – how promising is done, explicitly or inexplicitly, in words or by gestures, in words that themselves can, or cannot, be tagged as true or false. What it is is one question, and how it is done is another.

But if our proposition cannot simply be brushed aside by these objections, what is there to be said for it? Well, suppose we

---

[1] What I say here expresses an orthodox view, but I am not by any means confident that it is a correct one. It has been orthodox to hold that one who says 'I promise' does not therein say *that* he promises, or *that* anything else, and so – whatever he may convey – says nothing true or false. But why would it be wrong to hold that, in explicitly promising, he says – truly or falsely – *that* he promises? This however is a question about the workings of language, not promising, and accordingly need not be here pursued.

take it that in saying 'I will' I am, as suggested, not merely expressing an intention, but uttering (and conveying, as I might also have done otherwise) a genuine affirmation, in the real future tense, about my own future behaviour. Now, if this is subject to the requirement of truth, what follows? Plainly, it follows that I must actually act as I have said I will. It is for me, since it is in my power, *up* to me, to *make* my utterance true; and this of course I can do only by *doing* what I have said I will do. The case is quite different from that of an expression of an intention. Here, as we have seen, I do not really speak falsely, in saying 'I will', provided that, when I say so, I really mean to; my utterance has primarily to fit, as we put it, my present intention, and in so far as *thus* saying 'I will' comes close to saying 'I mean to', nothing necessarily is wrong – *very* wrong – if in future I do not in fact do what I said I was going to do. I am allowed, so to speak, simply to change my mind, without my original utterance thereby coming under (much) fire; for it was not in a sense, not primarily, about the future, and so is invulnerable, comparatively and except for special reasons, to future contingencies. But if I offer *as true* an affirmation about my future conduct, then I will have spoken falsely not *merely* if I do not now intend so to act, but *also* if in future I do not in fact act accordingly; so thereafter I *must* act, if I am not *to have* spoken falsely.

But, you will say, to speak falsely is not necessarily to speak culpably. That is true in general, and true in this case as well. But it is interesting to consider what exactly the position is here. There are two ways (at least) in which I may be more or less culpable in making an ordinary assertion that is actually false; I am culpable, first, if, in saying this is how things are, I do not actually believe that this is how things are; and I am culpable also, second, if, in saying this is how things are, I have not done as much as I could or reasonably should have done to ascertain that things actually are as I believe and assert them to be, that I am not misrepresenting things. Conversely, I am not culpable, even though I speak falsely, if I believe, though mistakenly, that things are as I say they are, and have done what I could or reasonably should have done in trying, though unsuccessfully, to ascertain how things actually are. This applies, of course, also to the special case of predictions. If I predict that I shall be bald by the age of fifty, I speak properly if I believe that that is what the future holds in store for me, and have considered such evidence as may seem to bear on the question; I am not culpable *merely* because I turn out to be wrong, for in such cases the future, as we more or less gloomily await its deliverances, is notoriously liable to come up with surprises. But now what if, having said, in the real future tense, that I will do X, I do not actually do it? What if I foretell, not just my own future, but my future *actions*? There are close and interesting analogues here. Again, there are two ways, it seems, in which I may be culpable. Firstly, I may have spoken, not believing at that time what I said – which must mean, since it is my own future conduct that is in question, that at that time I did not *intend* to act as I said I would; I did not, that is, believe that what I said was true, since, its truth being in my power, I did not mean to *make* it true. Second, I am culpable also, as in the former case, if, as one may put it, I do not take enough trouble to ensure that what I say does not misrepresent things – which in this case, since it is the utterance that comes *first* and its truth is up to me, will mean that thereafter I do not take enough trouble, do not do all that I could or reasonably should do, to make things so go that my utterance *did* not misrepresent them. But I am *not* culpable, here as in the former case, if, believing that what I say is true, that is, intending to *make* it true, I do all that I could or reasonably should do, even though unsuccessfully, to ensure that my utterance corresponds to the way things are – if, that is, having said that I will do X, I make such efforts as I can or reasonably should to do it. And here I cannot, of course, non-culpably, just change my mind; for to do that is simply to make my utterance false, and not excusably false; for if I change my mind, I have obviously *not* done what I could to make my utterance true. I have given up trying to, or possibly not even tried.

What, then, are we to say is the nature of the obligation invoked, when it is held that I ought to do X 'because I said I would'? Well, if I am right, it seems simply to be the requirement of *veracity*. What makes this unobvious, I think (if it *is* unobvious) is that, in the case of promising, the picture is, if one may put it so, the opposite way round to that with which, where veracity is concerned, one is most familiar, and of which – for that reason no doubt – one most naturally thinks. It is natural to think – since this is the familiar case – that what truthfulness requires is that words should be properly accommodated to the way things *are*; if the cat is on the mat, then what veracity requires of me is, supposing of course that I have occasion to go on about it at all, that I should produce such words as to affirm that the cat is on the mat. If we observe, however, that the essential requirement here is that, speaking rather informally, the words and the way things are should 'correspond', it may strike us that there is no particular reason for confining our attention to, so to speak, one direction, or 'sense', of this relationship – to the case, that is, in which the way things are (or were) is taken as given, and the requirement is that the words should be adjusted to that. For it is equally possible – since we can talk about the future – for the words to come first; and in that case what is required, if truth is to be satisfied, is that *things* should be conformed to the way the words previously were. If the cat is on the mat, then I speak truly (on that subject) only if I say that the cat is on the mat; but if I say that I will, meaning thereby not merely that I mean to but that I *will*, then I *have* spoken truly only if I subsequently *do*. And it surely does not matter if I say, not 'I will', but 'I promise'; for to say 'I promise' is of course to convey that I will, and moreover is to make it formally, explicitly clear that I am not just conveying that I mean to, but that I *will*. Colloquial English, at any rate, is perfectly aware of the position here; for the colloquial expression 'Take my word for it' is perfectly appropriate both to the situation where you are to take it that my words are properly accommodated to the way things actually are, and to that in which you are to take it that my subsequent actions will be properly accommodated to the way my words already have been. Truth, colloquial usage thus recognizes, is at stake in both cases.

The main burden of what I have to say on this subject could be summarized, I think, as the contention that we ought not – at least in the context of moral philosophy – to get into the habit of thinking of promising as somehow a *special case*, in need of some quite special explanation unique to itself. For to promise is to say something, and thereby to give something or other to be understood; and such a performance is surely subject to the quite general requirement that one should not, in speaking, give that to be understood which one does not think to be so or *to be going* to be so, or with respect to which one has not taken or *will not* take proper steps to ensure correspondence between words and things. Where things are given, the constraint, so to speak, falls on the words; where the words come first, the constraint falls on the speaker's future actions. The reason why I should *do* what I have said I *will* do is thus, in my submission, essentially the same as the reason why I should *say* I have done what I actually *have* done. How promising is done, or exactly how and why certain utterances are taken as promises, are – in the context of moral philosophy – relatively secondary questions; here, it is what promising *is* that counts, and why promising 'commits' the speaker to subsequent performance. And incidentally, if hackles rise too high at the proposition that promises are *predictions*, I would happily regard the latter – admittedly rather provocative – word as dispensable. What we are talking about matters; what label we attach to it does not.

We said at an earlier stage that, while the obligation of a promise does not wholly consist in the promise-maker's being 'counted on' to act in a certain way, it is not just irrelevant that he typically is so counted on. There is a bit more to be said as to the relevance of this consideration.

First, we have not hitherto had anything to say about the fact that a promise – not, I think, just typically, but always – is made, or given, to some recipient. Thus, I may promise my anxious parent that I will give up smoking, or my publisher to let him have my manuscript by a certain date. (The recipient, of course, is not necessarily *one* person, nor perhaps very exactly specified in any way – I may promise my whole body of employees a Christmas bonus, or perhaps, on television, make political promises to the electorate at large, of which I merely hope that some reasonable sample is viewing my performance.) Now, what is it to make a promise *to* a particular person? Well, I suppose that the person or persons to whom a promise is made will be those who have an *interest* in the doing of the thing promised (though doubtless others may have an interest in that as well); I would not, perhaps scarcely could, promise *you* that I will give up smoking, if you do not care a straw whether I give up smoking or not. Accordingly, to direct a promise, so to speak, *at* a particular person, is to convey that that person in particular, having an interest in the matter, may count upon the performance specified. Of course, just as you may acquire information from me though I am not talking *to* you when I give that information, so you may come to count on my acting in a certain way though it is not actually you that I authorize to count upon it. But here there is the special point that, if you are not the person *to* whom my promise was given, you cannot reasonably count upon the performance specified quite so confidently as you would have been entitled to do, if the promise had actually been made to you. This is for the reason that, since the object of a promise is to give to the person to whom it is made, the particular person who is known to have a relevant interest in the matter, assurance that the specified performance will actually be forthcoming, it is *open* to that person, the person whose interest is concerned, subsequently to indicate, if for any reason he sees fit to do so, that performance is not in fact required after all. I can thus, as we say, be 'released' from a promise I have made – but only, of course, by the person to whom I have made it, since, his re-assurance being the object of the exercise, it is for *him* to say whether or not he continues to require it. Thus, if I have not made my promise to you, you may without grounds for complaint be disappointed of the anticipated performance; for I may be 'released' from my promise by the person I made it to. The recipient of the promise is the person *for whose sake*, though not necessarily the only person to whose advantage, I am by my actions to make true what I convey in promising; if he comes not to want me to do so, it is for him to say.

That one who promises is, typically, counted on subsequently to perform may be relevant also in a different way. For to enable one person to count on some specified performance by another is after all, as we said at the outset, the object of the exercise, even though that he does so count on it is not the essential basis of the promise-maker's obligation. But if so, it must surely be allowed to make some difference if, for any reason, the recipient of a promise turns out actually *not* to be counting on its fulfilment at all. There are various possibilities here; we shall instance two. Suppose first that, having promised to feed your cat while you are away, I find that, when I go round to your house with my tins and milk-bottles, the cat's needs have already been supplied by some other hand. I may conclude, let us suppose correctly, that you have simply forgotten that I had promised to do the job, have made other arrangements, and thus of course are not counting on me to feed the cat at all. Rather differently, suppose that I have promised to lend you a certain book, but happen to learn, before I have actually conveyed it to you, that you have come by a copy of the same book from some other source – that is, you no longer need my copy of the book, and thus, though you may still be expecting it, are not *depending* on it. Well, what is the position here? It is, is it not, that, while I have promised to do something, and if I do not do it will not have done what 'I said I would', there is not, in the circumstances, the *point* in my doing it that there usually would be. For what is the point in my doing what I told you I would, if you are not expecting, or do not need, me to do it? Is it in any way culpable, then, not to keep a promise that there is, as it may turn out, no point in one's keeping? I do not really see how one could sensibly hold that this is culpable. At the same time, it seems that we are (in less trivial cases) disposed sometimes to *admire* even wholly pointless fidelity to undertakings; and, in so far as one ought to do what it is admirable to do, there may be cases in which one ought to do what one has said one would, even if there is not the usual point, or perhaps even any point, in one's doing it. Perhaps it is a good thing to be that sort of person – to be 'a man of one's word' *even* in situations in which it is *otherwise* not important that the thing should be done.

Let us now look back to the point from which, at the end of the last chapter, this discussion was launched. If one considers the situations in which we may raise the question what, from the moral point of view, we ought to do, one may be inclined at first to say that such situations can be distinguished into two classes. There is the kind of situation in which, free and uncommitted, we consider what, morally speaking, there is reason to do or not do, what the moral pros and cons are of the various options before us; our business is to identify the, morally, best thing to do. But then, one may think, there is the different kind of situation which one comes to already *committed* in some definite way, where what one ought to do is just that which one is committed to doing. Now there is no doubt, of course, that these situations are different; but it is not clear exactly what the difference consists in. One may think that it is, in a sense, a real difference of kind – in the one sort of situation, I am carefully to consider the merits of the case, in order to determine what is the best thing to do, whereas, in the other, perhaps I am not to raise *this* sort of question at all; perhaps it is irrelevant to ask what would be the best thing to do, or what may be the merits of the case, since what I ought to do is just what I am committed to doing. To be so committed is precisely *not* to be in a position to do what one may think, on the whole, would be the best thing to do, or what seems the best thing in the light of the merits of the case. On this sort of view, having reason to do this or that, or to judge that one ought to, is *one* kind of thing; having an *obligation* is something of a totally different kind.

But I think we can now see reason for rejecting this view of the matter; the difference here in question is not really a difference of that sort. For surely it is not that, where I have an obligation – where, for instance, I have made a promise – I am simply not to consider, when the situation arises in which fulfilment of my obligation falls due, anything *in* that situation *except* my obligation; I am not wholly to dismiss 'the merits of the case' from my attention. What is true, no doubt, is that it would be somewhat idle and irrelevant to consider what the merits of the case would suggest that I ought to do, if I had come to it without any antecedent obligation at all; nor can I properly, of course, just disregard my obligation in now considering what I ought to do. Still, an obligation surely is a reason for acting *among others*; and while no doubt it will often be rightly considered a preponderant reason, it can scarcely be supposed that it absolutely always will be, or that all other considerations are simply to be disregarded. It can be seen, in fact, that what we have said here about the obligation of a promise actually implies that other considerations are to be taken into account. For we said that one who has said that he will do something X (meaning that *he will*), if he is not to have spoken culpably falsely, must take such steps to make his words true (to 'make them good') as he can and *reasonably should*; and this is to imply, of course, that he is properly to consider whether doing X, when the time comes, is a thing that he should reasonably do, or whether there may not be reason why he should not do it. The position – looking back to an earlier stage of our discussion – could be put in this way. By promising to do X, by saying that I *will*, I bring it about that I will certainly have *a* reason for doing X, when the time comes; namely, I bring it about that *only* doing X will enable me to comply with the principle of truth (non-deception). We saw, however, that there are other moral principles than this one, and therefore other sorts of 'moral reasons' why one ought or ought not to do things; we saw also that reasons may conflict, point in opposite directions, and that one cannot say in general that, where conflict arises, any one principle is necessarily to predominate over others. If so, it is quite clear that, where I have an obligation – that is, *a* reason for acting in a definite way determined by the requirements of the principle of truth – there may be *other* reasons why I should *not* act in that way, and that those other reasons may sometimes be found preponderant. We may thus say that I am to consider, in *all* cases, 'the merits of the case', to see what reasons there are why I ought to do this or that, and so what, in the end, I ought to do. What is special about the obligation case is that I *start* here, so to speak, with a particular kind of reason – a reason that 'binds' me, in a quite determinate way, by specifying precisely the *only* thing I can do that, in the light of my words, will meet the requirements of truth. But still this reason, and that principle, must always go into the scales along with others; and I have no business to say, until I have considered the merits of the case, that, having *that* reason for doing X, X is what I ought to do. And after all there is nothing particularly startling in this; for I dare say we might have agreed at the very beginning that sometimes one ought not to keep a promise one has made. Perhaps, for instance, I ought not to keep a promise I have made to you, if to do so would be grossly unjust towards somebody else, or grossly damaging to some quite legitimate interest of his. Truth may compete with justice or non-maleficence, and may sometimes lose.

I must try, finally, briefly to make good my earlier suggestion that obligations in general can be construed more or less on the model of the obligation of promises. In fact this can, I believe, rather easily be made out. With promising, the essence of the case as here presented is that, by my words, I give it to be understood that I will act in a certain way; and thereafter, if truth is to be satisfied, I must so act – there is something which, by my own words, I am 'bound' to doing. All we need now, I think, to take in obligation in general, is to recognize that one may give it to be understood that one will act in a certain way, not by words, but by actions. (In fact, there is in a sense no contrast here at all, since saying the things that I say is *among* the things that I do.) There are, of course, degrees of explicitness here, and degrees of determinacy, and also, importantly, degrees of awareness and forethought. It is pretty explicitly laid down, for instance, what a tutorial Fellow of an Oxford college is required to do; it is thus pretty definite what obligations I incur, what exactly I give it to be understood that I will do, in accepting election as a tutorial Fellow. But there is, I suppose, a much less definite understanding as to what is expected of a host, or a guest, or a foreign visitor; and it is therefore less clear just what obligations are incurred by putting oneself, or being put, in those situations. And it is important that whereas, with explicit, actual promising, I can scarcely be unaware what it is that I am giving it to be understood that I will do, and hence exactly what obligation it is that I am incurring, it is quite easy to commit oneself by one's actions without really foreseeing – very often, no doubt, because one prefers not to foresee – just what obligations one incurs thereby. No doubt, if I have given something to be understood – for instance, that I will marry my landlord's daughter – by pure inadvertence or misapprehension – being simply unaware, for instance, that to shake a girl's right hand is the way, in this society, formally to signify betrothal –

I could cogently maintain that I have incurred no obligation at all; for I certainly did not mean what I am thus taken to have meant, and could not have been expected to know that I would be so taken. But if, as often happens, I simply do not think – do not attend, though I quite well could, to what my intentional conduct is certainly going to convey – then, I may, surely, find that I have really incurred obligations which I never clearly intended to incur, or admitted to incurring.

But the principle in all cases, I believe, is exactly the same; what is at stake, in each case, is the preservation of truth. We often so speak or so act that, if we are not to *have* spoken or acted falsely, with mendacity, we *must* act thereafter in some more or less determinate way. It is thus, in my submission, that our words and our acts – indeed, even some things that we merely *allow* to occur – may 'bind' us for the future; they make it the case that *only* by acting in a certain way can we ensure that we *did* not, earlier, speak or act falsely.

8. Marginal Comments

In this penultimate chapter I take up a handful of issues which, while not really central to anything I particularly wish to say, are perhaps too firmly entrenched in the subject to be passed over altogether. I shall say a little about the relation of morality to knowledge; rather more about the language of morals, so far as there is such a thing; and finally, a very little on the relation of morality to religion.

(A) MORALITY AND KNOWLEDGE

Are there moral facts? Are there sentences that can be held to express moral propositions? If we say that there are, are we ready to swallow the evident consequence that the terms 'true' and 'false' could be properly applied in such contexts? And if so, what about the further apparent consequence that, in morality, knowledge could in principle be claimed? For where we have propositions that can be true or false, we have at least the possibility of *knowing* that something is so, or not so. Is there moral knowledge?

Well, no doubt these are not clear questions, but one thing is undeniable; and that is, that common usage comes down decisively on one side of this fence. If I were to say that, for instance, Goebbels in his time did some morally abominable things, no eyebrows would ordinarily be raised if you were to reply with 'That's true'; and if you should happen to think that Goebbels was a much maligned politician, who in fact conscientiously did his best in very difficult circumstances, it would be quite natural for you to say of my remark 'That's not true'. We often say – even philosophers often say – that people sometimes do things 'knowing' that what they are doing is wrong; or we may say of some moral delinquent, for one reason or another, that he 'knows no better' – he does not know, though of course others do, that his behaviour is wrong. Certainly, then, if we are to take common usage as a guide, there *are* moral propositions, moral truths and falsehoods; and, given such a proposition, we may sometimes know that it is true, or be unaware that it is true, or wonder whether it is really true or not, and so on.

But this need not, of course, be accepted as at all decisive. A philosopher who wishes to hold that there are not really any moral propositions, that there cannot really be such a thing as knowledge, or truth and falsehood, in moral matters, can argue that common usage is not to be taken seriously here – it is, he may say, just misleading, or confused, or positively *wrong* perhaps. Nor is it difficult, if one wishes to hold that common usage is here infelicitous, to construct a hypothesis to explain how this might have come about. Moral utterances, one may say, have at least two features in common with others that really are propoundings of propositions – features which make it entirely natural to assume that in general they are very much alike, and consequently, uncritically, to speak as if that were so. For one thing, there are obvious and extensive grammatical analogies; the sentences people produce in their moral utterances may have subjects and predicates, and verbs in the indicative mood, exactly like sentences which really do express propositions, and, grammatically, they can be negated and otherwise operated upon in just the same ways. The sentences 'Snow is white' and 'Snow is not white' really do express propositions; and they not only look just like, but perhaps, grammatically, really are just like, the sentences, for instance, 'Lying is wrong' and 'Lying is not wrong'. Differently, perhaps it may be thought even more insidiously, there are psychological similarities between moral utterances and the propoundings of real propositions. When we propound a real proposition, assert some fact, we often do so with great assurance; we may have absolute confidence in the rightness of what we say, even think it completely obvious that we are right; we may think it important that other people should agree with us, and be ill at ease, or sharply critical of them, if they do not do so. And we may justify these feelings or attitudes, to ourselves or others, by the reflection that what we say, after all, is just true, is a fact and, perhaps, an obvious fact, and should be recognized as such. But now,

people issue moral utterances with no less assurance; here too
they feel sure that they are right, even obviously right, and that
others will or at any rate should agree with what they say. But if
so, it is wholly understandable that they should come to speak
as if they had, for these feelings and attitudes, the same warrant
as in the former case; and it may even be that, exactly in proportion as they do not really have it, they will speak more ag-
gressively and emphatically as if they had. They will claim truth
for what they say, and that they *know* that it is true. They will
disparage dissenters as simply mistaken on the facts. They will
probably come actually to believe, in some inexplicit, unfor-
mulated way, that moral rightness and wrongness are as much
factual features of the world as are colours and shapes, and that
they actually 'see' them there, so that their moral utterances
really are just truths about the world, some anyway quite obviously true to the attentive observer. But this, it might be urged,
though wholly natural, is still an illusion; even the sharpest eyes
do not really *see* moral properties; to come to speak in this way,
perhaps even to think in this way, is to project one's own cer-
tainies, one's confidently held moral sentiments, onto the world,
and to take for real features of the world what are only the
shadows cast over it by one's inner convictions.[1] So, people may
indeed talk thus; but such talk, from the standpoint of ethics,
need not be taken seriously.

But why should it not be? It would be tedious and unfruit-
ful, I think, to go into this at great length; moral philosophers
have spent already a good deal too much time in the unreward-
ing (for ethics) polemics of epistemology. But I believe that the
feeling that has led many people to conclude that there cannot
be moral facts, moral truths and falsehoods, moral knowledge,
could be said in a general way to be the feeling that moral questions are not sufficiently *objective*, or perhaps are not objective at
all. Why, briefly, might one feel this?

Most crudely, one might for a start be tempted to say that
those only are genuinely objective features of the world which
we can, almost literally, *see* there – the presence or absence of

[1] In Hume's pleasing phrase (*Treatise*, I, sec. XIV), ''tis a common observation, that the mind has a great propensity to spread itself on external
objects'.

which can be decisively established by the senses, by observation, aided perhaps by such unproblematic, re-assuringly impersonal procedures as measurement or counting. But this does not take us very far. For what, we may ask, is supposed to be importantly distinctive about what is 'objective' in this rather crude sense? Presumably it is that, for an objective feature P, whether something is P or is not can in principle be definitely *settled*; there is a right answer to the question, that can be shown to be right to the satisfaction of any (competent, impartial, careful, etc.) observer. But then there is a great *variety* of questions of which this much is true; for instance, in law, or in history, or in logic and mathematics, while something more is involved than just observation, use of the eyes or ears, or even of instruments – here we have to think, or argue, judgement must be exercised – nevertheless there are questions – *some* questions – that can be quite definitely settled. Might such questions, then, not be quite properly recognized as objective, even though they are not concerned, or not merely concerned, with the presence or absence of strictly *observable* features?

But even so, it will be said – even if we extend the honorific title of 'objective' beyond the limits of the strictly observable – there remains plain reason to insist that *moral* questions are not objective. Consider only how people differ on these matters, notoriously; could one be sure of producing *any* 'proposition' in morals that would not be found affirmed by many, denied by many, and no doubt by many never entertained at all? If there were really any way of settling such questions decisively, how could it be that none (perhaps) ever gets decisively settled? Is it not more reasonable to take the view that people just differ on these questions, adopt different attitudes, feel differently about them, and that if they think, as they often will, that some are *right* and others *wrong* by some objective criterion, then they are the victims of a natural, but total, illusion? Should we not say that, on moral matters, people are free to make up their own minds, even required to make up their own minds, in a sense that fully allows for the possibility that they will end up thinking *differently*, and that that is all that can be said?

This, however, is hasty. We may note for a start that, on any question at all, people after all are 'free' to make up their own minds – how indeed, on any question, could somebody *else* make up *my* mind? Nor perhaps, on any non-trivial question, do we seriously expect to find universal agreement. It is, of course, obviously true that people differ, have differed and doubtless will differ, enormously over questions of right and wrong – the *scale* of dissension here may be uncommonly large; but there may, surely, be many reasons why this should be so. Sometimes it may be that people are not putting to themselves quite the same question – one who pronounces that X is morally wrong may be considering X-in-circumstances-A, one who 'differs' is thinking of X-in-circumstances-B; they *might* take the *same* view of X in just the same circumstances. Or again, they may not be employing quite the same concepts – and one who says that X is morally wrong is not contradicted by one who says that it is not wrong, not using moral concepts at all. (If I say that X is a crime in English law, you do not contradict me by saying that, in French law, it is not.) Very often, no doubt, the issue cannot be definitely settled – but this may *often* be because the issue is not at all a simple one, may call for information that actually we have not got, for foreknowledge that we could not possibly have, perhaps for insight and judgement with which not all are equally well-endowed, or for some balancing of pros and cons that will inevitably be inconclusive. The fact is that one needs to do a good deal of work to get, from the undoubted datum of extensive difference, to the conclusion that the issues are all ultimately *subjective* – that is, rest on something like tastes or personal choices, in which people just differ and are perfectly 'free' to do so.

But the best way, no doubt, to show that this is really not so would be actually to produce a plain specimen of a moral truth, some moral proposition that can be definitely shown to be true. I will accordingly do so. Suppose that I am dictator of some state or other, greatly enjoying the pleasures and perquisites of untrammelled despotism. One day, to my chagrin, I learn from my secret agents that some high-minded university professors, appalled at the cruelty and oppressiveness of my régime, are considering forcing upon me abdication of my power, and a more or less honourable but unexciting seclusion in some quiet rural area. I sagaciously hesitate to court unpopularity by proceeding directly to their destruction, and accordingly devise a less overt scheme to secure my position against them. I decide to have my ambassador in a neighbouring state assassinated, to use this pretext to appeal to the nationalist passions of my subjects, and in due course to rally the populace solidly behind me in actual war upon the adjacent victim; once that is well under way, it will be quite easy to fabricate evidence representing my critics as unpatriotic, even traitors in the national crisis, and then they can be liquidated in perfect security. I disclose my scheme to my confidant, perhaps with some pride in my ingenuity; and he observes 'What you propose to do is morally wrong'.

Now this is not really deniable, and can be – though it scarcely needs to be – conclusively shown. The course that I propose involves assassination for a start and something like judicial murder to finish up with; it involves a great deal of lying and fabrication of evidence; it involves the gratuitous death and wanton injury of large numbers of inoffensive persons, and no doubt a great deal of destruction and damage to their property; and what I urge in favour of this course of action is that it will secure to me personally certain pleasures and powers which I greatly enjoy. This description of the situation is not contestable; and it is not contestable that a course of action so describable conflicts grossly with most, or even all, principles of morality, and cannot possibly be credited with any counterbalancing *moral* justification. Now of course you are free, in some sense, not to accept this conclusion – that is, you can deny it (as Oscar Wilde noted, one can deny anything). You can allege that my project does *not* conflict with any of the principles suggested, the only drawback to this allegation being that it is manifestly false. Or you can hold that, though it does conflict with them, it is not morally wrong – but in that case, what could you be taking 'morally wrong' to *mean*? Just as to hold that snow is not white would be evidence for supposing that one did not know what 'white' means, to hold that this course of action was not morally wrong cold only suggest ignorance of the meaning of 'morally wrong'.

It is important to be clear as to what the suggestion is here. It could *of course* be held that what I propose is not wrong; for it is quite possible to think that a man is absolutely right to do anything whatever that serves his own ends and interests, and even to admire the ingenious ruthlessness with which he may do so. To triumph thus over one's enemies, one may think, is absolutely splendid. But what one cannot think is that this is not *morally* wrong. Why not? Well, if the phrase 'morally wrong' is not absolutely meaningless; if it is possible to say, in elucidation of what it means, what sorts of things rank semantically as morally wrong; then there are some things, such as those described, from which that appellation *could* not be withheld by anyone not unaware of the meaning of the expression, or not deliberately misusing it. Accordingly, that *some* things anyway are morally wrong can be shown to be true, every bit as decisively, as incontestably, as it can be shown to be true that, for instance, snow is white. But if, as seems reasonable, the question whether some sort of issues is 'objective' is made to turn on the question whether pronouncements on those issues can ever be shown decisively to be true or false, we have reason here for saying that moral issues can be objective. There are *some* moral truths and falsehoods, some moral knowledge. Possibly not much in fact; but some in principle, and (let us be sensible about it) some in fact as well. In some cases, we know that moral propositions are true, exactly as we know anything else – that is, we know in general what the conditions would be for correct application of some, say, moral predicate, and we find instances in which we know that those conditions are satisfied. This is, as we have noted, the style in which we ordinarily talk; and I can see no good reason why we should not talk in that way.

That is all that, in this connection, I really wish to contend for. Of course it is true that 'moral qualities' are not objective features of the world in the sense that they are 'there' quite independently of people; if there were no rational beings, there would be no moral facts. Equally, it is true, as we have admitted, that one cannot suppose that to every moral question there must *be* – objectively, whether we can know it or not – a definite answer; for where it is a matter of balancing pros and cons, it may be that, even if we were perfectly judicious and perfectly informed, we might find that the balance did not tip decisively either way. But it is *not* true that every moral question is 'a matter of opinion', still less a matter of taste, or personal preference, or choice. That lying, murder, and violence for the sake of my private pleasures is morally wrong is a proposition that I may, of course, view with complete indifference. I may even think it right to do what is morally wrong. I can of course deny that proposition, refuse to admit it, as I can, if sufficiently brazen, deny anything at all. However, the proposition is true, and not disputably so. Since morality is not after all a quite meaningless term, nor a term to which one is at liberty to attach any private sense that one may fancy, some things are, as one may put it, morally wrong *by definition*.[1] No doubt not very many, nor of course in difficult, obscure, or very complicated cases; but *some* things, in this field, we know. I think we *know* that we do.

(B) MORALITY AND LANGUAGE

The thesis that I wish to argue for on this topic is, negatively and perhaps disappointingly, that there is really nothing special, or specially illuminating, about the *language* of moral discourse. Such discourse is, no doubt, sometimes linguistically distinguishable from other sorts of talk, but only, I think, in the not very profound way in which talk on any subject is naturally likely to be distinguishable from talk on any other – that is, by reference to its vocabulary. There are, for instance, certain *words* – 'state', 'authority', 'rights', 'sovereignty', 'government', and so on – which typically and perhaps inevitably occur in talking or writing about politics; and for that reason a book of some years ago, whose subject was the critical analysis of political concepts, was appropriately and accurately called *The Vocabulary of Politics*.[2] In the same way no doubt moral discourse has its vocabulary – some words which, because of what they mean, would suggest at any rate *prima facie* that discourse in which they occurred was about matters of morality; but at the same time it should be remembered, of course, that a very great deal even of the vocabulary in which moral matters are discussed is actually not proprietary to moral matters. Such terms as 'good', 'bad', 'right', 'wrong', 'ought', and 'duty', even 'virtue' and 'obligation', do not

[1] By definition, that is, of *morality*, not, uninterestingly, of the actions themselves.
[2] By T. D. Weldon (Penguin Books, 1953).

necessarily indicate that *moral* matters are under discussion; for of course there are virtues that are not moral virtues, duties that are not moral duties, good things that are not morally good, and so on. Still, just as physicists make use of some items of vocabulary that are peculiar to the discussion of physics, lawyers of some terms of art peculiar to law, and so on, so doubtless there are *some* terms used by moralists and others that are, as items of vocabulary, peculiar to moral discourse. What seems to me not true, though it seems to have been widely believed, is that there is in any other sense a 'use of language' that is distinctive of moral discourse, and therefore capable of illuminating moral concepts, or the concept of morality. That this should have come to be believed is, I think, historically understandable; a brief excursus at this point into recent history may be helpful.

Let us take for consideration some sentence, utterance of which might well constitute the making of a moral judgement, and let us assume that, as considered here, it actually would do so – the sentence, say, 'Tax-dodging is wrong'. Now one possible view of utterances of that sort, though perhaps never a very popular one at any rate in its simplest form, is that such utterances are purely 'subjective' – in saying 'Tax-dodging is wrong', a speaker simply *means* that he himself has some unfavourable feeling about, or attitude towards, the practice of tax-dodging. However, it has been very commonly supposed, and rightly, that this will hardly do as it stands – if only because, if this were right, to 'support' his remark that tax-dodging was wrong a speaker would need only to establish that he did in fact have an unfavourable feeling or attitude towards that practice, and could do so of course quite *consistently* with someone else's dictum that tax-dodging was not wrong: that Smith feels unfavourably towards the practice of tax-dodging is perfectly consistent with the proposition that Jones does not. Most philosophers, I think, have been disposed, reasonably and rightly, to make the supposition that the utterances 'Tax-dodging is wrong' and 'Tax-dodging is not wrong', provided of course that each utterer is making a moral judgement, and a moral judgement about the same thing, express inconsistent, directly (in *some* way) conflicting moral judgements; this is what the verbal form of the sentences strongly suggests, and most have been ready to accept that very natural suggestion; and this seems to be to suppose that the judgement that tax-dodging is wrong says something *about* tax-dodging, asserts something to be true of it, which the contradictory judgement denies. There is room, of course, even so for substantial disagreement as to what it is that is said about tax-dodging in the assertion that it is wrong – that most people condemn it? that it has certain undesired consequences? that it has come indefinable *sui generis* character of wrongness? – but let us stick for the moment at the common, very natural supposition that to say that X is wrong is to say something about X, something offered as true of it, as a fact about it.

Now it began to be felt, somewhere about the year 1930, that this supposition, notwithstanding its wholly natural, innocent look and very general acceptance, must be in principle wrong, or at any rate that something essential must be missing from it. For if we say just this, can we, it was asked, make any sense at all of the relation of moral judgement to *action*? If 'Tax-dodging is wrong' just says something about tax-dodging, then one who utters those words is just stating a belief that he has, something that he takes to be the case; or perhaps, in stating that belief, his idea will be to purvey information to the person he is talking to, to tell him what the facts are, that something or other is the case. But surely this is wrong. If I am delivering a lecture, for instance, about owls, then indeed it may be the whole object of my discourse to set forth what I believe to be truths about owls, and to provide my audience with information about owls, some of which may, though of course not necessarily, be new to them. To be truthful, to be informative, may be all that I intend; I want my hearers to *know* some things about owls, but I may very well not want them to *do* anything in particular, whether about owls or anything else – my discourse may simply have nothing to do with anybody's conduct. But surely moral discourse is not like this at all. For here, on the contrary, the whole point of saying this or that is, not to add to or alter people's beliefs or information, but to make some practical difference in what people *do* – the *point* of pronouncing that tax-dodging is wrong is not just to get people to think, accept, believe something about tax-dodging, but to get them *not to do it*. But this essential element in the case, whatever exactly it may be, seems totally omitted from the naïve supposition that moral judgements express moral beliefs, and purvey information. This innocent-looking supposition, it was suggested, actually conceals the major mistake of overlooking the *practical* character of moral discourse – of representing that sort of talk as being merely, like some other sorts, fact-stating or 'descriptive', rather than as being directed, as surely it essentially is, to making an actual difference in what people do.

So how are things to be set right? Well, the suggestion has been made that what is needed is recognition of a special sort of *meaning,* and, in association with that, of a special 'use of language'. This suggestion has come in two versions.[1] According to the earlier version, what we need to recognize, in addition to 'descriptive' meaning, is 'emotive' meaning. A word like 'table' presumably has descriptive meaning only – there is a certain class of articles of furniture which are, in fact, properly to be said to be tables. Probably a word like 'Italian' also has descriptive meaning only – there are, quite simply, certain factual conditions for the correct application of that word. The word 'Wop', however, is a different matter, for while this no doubt has descriptive meaning – the same meaning, let us assume, as 'Italian' has – it also has a further feature: it standardly expresses a certain attitude of contempt for, or hostility towards, what it is applied to, and may tend to arouse a similar attitude in others. This is its emotive meaning. And thus also we get two different 'uses of language'. If I say 'Those people are Italian', my use of language may be said itself to be purely descriptive; I merely express, and perhaps convey, what I take to be a truth about those people. But if I say 'Those people are a bunch of Wops', my object is typically different, or at any rate is not merely that; my use of language expresses my contempt for those people, and probably has the 'dynamic' purpose of evoking an attitude of contempt in my hearers. Thus we have, associated with descriptive and emotive meaning, a descriptive and a 'dynamic' use of language. The essential link between moral discourse and action is then said to

[1] I have in mind here, as will be obvious, the 'emotivism' of C. L. Stevenson and the 'prescriptivism' of R. M. Hare. The classic texts are the former's *Ethics and Language* (Yale U. P., 1945) and the latter's *The Language of Morals* (O.U.P., 1952).

consist in the fact that moral discourse is a dynamic use; its object, and typically its effect, is to *influence* what people do by way of operating, causally, upon their feelings or 'attitudes'.

The more recent version, while not wholly dissimilar in its general character, differs nevertheless at both the crucial points. The special sort of meaning to be recognized, it suggests, is not emotive meaning, but 'prescriptive' meaning; and the use of language involved, while possibly to be called 'dynamic', is to be thought of not as a mode of causal influencing, but rather as what we may call 'imperatival guiding'. It is not that there is no such thing as emotive meaning, or that language cannot be or is not used merely to work psychologically upon the feelings of an audience; it is simply that it is not *this* that is interestingly distinctive of moral discourse. In the sentence 'Tax-dodging is wrong', is the predicate 'wrong' really an *emotive* word? And if I tell you that tax-dodging is wrong, am I essentially out to *cause* you to feel unfavourably towards that practice? Surely not. The word 'wrong', we may say, while not particularly if at all emotive, is a word that has *prescriptive* meaning – its use connotes that what it is applied to is *not to be done*; and accordingly my telling you that tax-dodging is wrong is properly to be assimilated, not to an attempt to work causally upon your feelings, but to telling you, imperatively, not to do it. And this gives us, of course, a different picture of the essential link between moral discourse and action. The 'use' of language here, while possibly dynamic, is not so merely in virtue of being causally efficacious; it is prescriptive; it has, overtly or indirectly, imperative force. Just as compliance with an order or instruction requires one to *do* something, so *actions* are consistent or inconsistent with moral utterances.

It seems to me, however, fairly luminously clear that this suggestion, in either version, is entirely wrong. The first version amounts essentially to this. In order, it is said, to supply the deficiencies of the naïve supposition that moral judgements express merely beliefs, or information, we ought to consider what is *done by* the issuing of such judgements; we must take note of the 'dynamic' purpose of the speaker in such cases; and this will bring to our notice the emotive character of the vocabulary employed. But this is wrong in at least two ways. In the first place, there is nothing at all that can be said to be *done by* the making of moral judgements as such. That the producer of moral dicta is not necessarily, not always, seeking to influence anybody will perhaps be obvious, if one reflects on the immense variety of situations and settings in which, and topics on which, moral dicta may be produced; that there is always one and the same purpose in view may well seem obviously false. But if that is not enough, one may reflect that moral judgements are not necessarily *spoken* at all; there is, after all, moral thinking as well as moral talking, and when in such a case I am, so to speak, my own audience, it seems rather worse than implausible to suppose that I am trying emotionally to sway that audience by working verbally upon its feelings. But in the second place, it is also obviously true that this 'use of language' – the use, that is, by a speaker of emotive language with the object, or for the purpose, of influencing the feelings of an audience – is not distinctive of moral discourse, even if it may sometimes occur therein. What has happened here, then, is that attention has really been switched to a quite different, much more general phenomenon – the use of language for the 'dynamic' purpose of influencing feelings. Now this does occur; but it has nothing in particular to do with morals. For moral judgements are certainly not always specimens of this use of language; and vastly many specimens of this use of language are not moral judgements. In this sense, there is *no* 'use' of language in moral discourse, as such.

But the revised version is off-target in a quite closely analogous way. Here the suggestion is that illumination is to be sought not from what is done *by* moral discourse, but from what is done *in* it – not from the speaker's purpose, but from the nature of his linguistic act; *prescribing* is to be the key. Now, in the first place, there develops something of a dilemma here. Just as, one may think, it was obviously absurd to suppose that one who engages in moral discourse has always some single purpose in view in doing so, we cannot surely suppose with any show of reason that there is some *one* kind of linguistic act which he always performs. Are there not dozens of distinguishable linguistic acts, *any* of which may be performed in moral discourse, as elsewhere? Thus, if 'prescribing' means anything in particular – as, for instance, 'telling somebody what to do' – it will be obvious that to engage in moral discourse is not necessarily to prescribe. But if, to avoid this obvious objection, we make the notion of prescribing so highly generic as not to be inapplicable to *any* linguistic act that may occur in moral discourse, do we really know any longer what 'prescriptive' means? Thus, in the first place, we seem to have here a character ascribed to acts of moral discourse in general, which either it is certain that some such acts do not have, or which is so generically omni-tolerant as to have no determinate sense. But in the second place, we surely have here once again a displacement of attention to some quite different, much more general phenomenon – the use of language in prescribing courses of action to people. This also does occur; but it also has nothing in particular to do with morals. For moral judgements in general can all be specimens of this use of language only if the notion of 'prescribing' is bemusingly stretched; and it is in any case certain that vastly many specimens of this use of language are not moral judgements. We prescribe in all sorts of fields, for all sorts of reasons; so that, in this sense also, there is *no* 'use' of language in moral discourse, as such.

What is it, then, that is distinctive of 'moral discourse'? How is it that we can tell, as presumably we more or less can, when we have a specimen or stretch of moral discourse before us? The obvious answer to this question seems to me to be the right one: we go by what that specimen or stretch of discourse is *about*. A political speech, for example, which is no doubt a specimen, though not the only species, of 'political discourse', is identified as such as by being found to be about politics – that is, about elections, votes, parties, governments, oppositions, programmes, public administration, or something of that sort. Whatever the speaker's object may be in speaking – whether he is exhorting, advising, condemning, excoriating, adulating, simply describing, or all of these or none – he is producing political discourse if he is talking about politics, political issues or affairs. Exactly similarly, it seems to me, moral discourse can be characterized in general only by saying that it must be about morals – discourse, conducted for some purpose or other and in some way or other,

about some moral issue or matter. But how do we tell that some
tract of discourse *is* 'about' morals? Well, that may not be easy.
If the tract of discourse we are considering is a fairly extensive
one, then it is quite likely that one could identify it as *moral*
discourse on the basis of its vocabulary. Just as certain words, as
we have seen – 'state', 'authority', 'rights', 'sovereignty', 'government', and so on – may be said to belong to the vocabulary of
politics, and so might, if they crop up often enough and in appropriate ways, identify some tract of discourse as broadly about
politics, we might sometimes identify some tract of discourse
as about morals by the appropriate occurrence in it of certain
words – 'unjust' perhaps, 'cruelty', 'deceitful', 'honest', or
'generous', and, of course, 'moral', 'morally', 'morality' themselves. However, as we pointed out earlier, a great deal of the
vocabulary in which moral matters are discussed is not at all
peculiar to discussion of those matters; so that, particularly if
our tract of discourse is a fairly short one, there may be no words
in it that show it to be 'about' morals. So what would be the
further evidence that we should then need? We should need, I
think, essentially some information as to the *grounds on which*
things said in that tract of discourse were said. If you say to me
that Smith ought not to have acted as he did, I cannot tell from
your words – since there is nothing peculiarly moral about
'ought' – whether or not you are making a moral comment;
but it would become clear that you were, if you went on to back
up your remark about Smith with appropriate reasons, that is,
with moral reasons. And similarly if, in words not peculiarly
moral, you had offered advice or commendation, expressed regret or disapproval, or something of that sort. Moral discourse,
then, can be and should be identified by its subject-matter or
topic; and what the subject-matter or topic is, may sometimes
be revealed by some items of the vocabulary employed, or, alternatively or additionally, by the sort of grounds on which things
said in such discourse are or would be supported. Nothing in
particular, however, can be said in general as to what such discourse is undertaken *for* – there is no purpose which the speaker
necessarily and always has in mind (except, trivially, that of engaging in moral discourse); neither can anything in particular
be said in general as to what is done *in* such discourse – there is

no 'speech act' which is necessarily and always performed (except, again trivially, that of utterance, and utterance of some item of moral discourse).

But, it may be objected, if one takes this line, surely one has done nothing at all to answer the crucial question posed at an earlier stage – namely, the question how moral discourse is related, as surely it essentially is, to conduct. If we just say that moral discourse as such is 'about' a certain subject-matter or range of topics, do we not, as was objected earlier to some traditional doctrines, leave it wholly mysterious how remarks on those topics are related, or even could be related, to *practical* matters? But surely it must be allowed that moral discourse is, after all, meant to make a practical difference – not just to *tell* people things, but to bear in some essential way on what they actually do. But, as I hope will now be obvious, there is no great problem here. We have said that moral discourse is not undertaken, in general, for any *one* practical purpose, and also that no *one* speech act is performed therein which would relate, in some *one* way, what is said to practical matters. But this does not imply that the moral discourser has *no* practical purpose, or performs *no* speech act which relates what he says to practice. The truth of course is that, while such practical purposes and speech acts (if we may put it so) are not distinctive of moral discourse, and while no one in particular necessarily occurs there, there is a vast diversity of such that may *in fact* occur there. Discourse that is 'about' morals, that is, is moral discourse, may consist of or include advising – a performance which stands in one sort of relation to a practical question, and can (perhaps) be associated also with a typical sort of purpose; or reproving, which is related to action in a different way, and of which the object is different; or regretting, deploring, criticizing, appraising, undertaking, and so on and so on. Of course moral discourse is in a sense practical; for, as we said at the start, it has essentially to do, in varying degrees of directness, with a certain kind of evaluation of actions. But this tells us no more than, very vaguely, what it is about. It is quite wrong to infer from this that moral discourse as such bears some *single* relation to questions of conduct, or as such must be engaged in for some *single* sort of practical purpose. We can talk about what people do, or have done, or may do, or are going to do, for enormously many quite different purposes; we may be doing, in so talking, very many quite different things; and exactly *how* what we say is related to conduct, and to *whose* conduct, is a matter of exactly what, in this case or that, we are saying and (therein) doing. To those questions, there is no answer at all that can be derived from the mere datum that we are engaging in 'moral discourse'.

A question which might be raised here – and which also, fortunately, can be quite easily answered – is the question what it is about moral concepts in virtue of which they are *capable* of non-trivial occurrence in such a huge diversity of linguistic performances, or of being deployed for such a variety of practical purposes. What we have said in earlier chapters yields an answer to this question readily enough. There are, we suggested, certain fundamental *principles* of morality, the distinctive feature of which is that general observance of them would tend to ameliorate the human predicament, specifically by tending to countervail such ills as are liable to result from the limitedness of 'human sympathies'. In just that sense, there is reason for compliance with those principles, and reason against – to put it awkwardly – breach or neglect of them. Hence a 'moral reason' as previously defined – that is, a consideration tending to establish conformity or non-conformity with a moral principle – counts *for* or *against* (not necessarily conclusively) the doing of things; and moral concepts in general are applied, of course in ways that differ very widely in detail, on the basis of recognition and appraisal of moral reasons. But since we thus have, essentially, the general feature of considerations counting for or against the doing of things, it will be obvious that there arises the possibility of performing, with such concepts, a great diversity of speech acts – advising, in which one indicates that relevant considerations count *for* some contemplated course of action; reproof, in which one indicates that they count *against* some action or course of action already performed; condemnation; commendation; warning; regret; and so on. (Incidentally, considerations counting for or against certain courses of action of course *may* be deployed in advocating the formulation of, justifying compliance with, or criticizing breaches of, rules; but it is quite incidental that they may be deployed in this connection – that is, while, where rules are concerned, they must be so deployable, they are not deployed necessarily and only in relation to rules.) It can in fact be quite easily seen that, in consequence of the essential 'for or against' character of moral considerations, there can occur in moral discourse 'illocutionary forces' of *any* of the five general types which Austin (with admitted qualms) thought up general names for.[1] Obviously there will occur 'verdictives', which, in Austin's words, 'consist in the delivering of a finding, official or unofficial, upon evidence or reasons as to value or fact, so far as these are distinguishable'. Also 'exercitives' – 'the giving of a decision in favour of or against a certain course of action, or advocacy of it'. Then 'commissives' – the point of which is 'to commit the speaker to a certain course of action', with the consequence at least *prima facie* that he ought so to act. 'Behabitives' will occur also, which in various ways give expression to 'reaction to other people's behaviour and fortunes', or 'attitudes' towards their past conduct and imminent conduct. And lastly, of course, as in any sort of discourse, 'expositives', which involve 'the expounding of views, the conducting of arguments, and the clarifying of usages and of references'. It is worth noting here that Austin instances stating, denying, and describing as expositives; and that nothing, of course, which we have said in this paragraph is at all inconsistent with our previous suggestion that at least some moral utterances may be plain statements of truths, of moral propositions some of which can be *known* to be true. Such a statement, for that matter, can be *both* true *and*, for instance, a condemnation – rather as 'That's highly inflammable' can at one and the same time be true and, for instance, a warning.

This brief digression into the philosophy of language has been undertaken here, not because I believe that the philosophy of language has much positive contribution to offer to moral philosophy, but for the negative reason that, in my opinion, moral philosophy in our day has been substantially obfuscated by rather complex confusions in the philosophy of language. It may possibly have been supposed by old-school moral philosophers

---

[1] See *How to Do Things with Words* (O.U.P., 1962), pp. 148–162.

K

(though the evidence that this *was* supposed is not actually very good) that utterances in moral discourse, or at any rate the only ones deserving of serious attention, were essentially just *statements*, propoundings as true of moral propositions. Well, if they did suppose that, they were certainly in error; there is no reason to deny that some utterances in moral discourse are (and even, are just) statements, but certainly there are many such utterances, by no means neglect-worthy, which are not propoundings as true of anything at all. So that was, or would have been, an error; but what seems to have occurred is that its successive critics condemned it on quite the wrong grounds. It seems to have been supposed in the first place, wrongly, that, if one takes a certain specimen or species of discourse to consist wholly or essentially of propoundings of propositions, this commits one also to the further supposition that such discourse can incorporate only one 'use of language', either in the sense of having only one *purpose*, or in that of having only one sort of illocutionary force. Thus it seems to have been assumed, wrongly, that if some utterance propounds a proposition, the speaker can *only* have the purpose of 'informing', and his act can *only* be that of, say, 'stating', or 'describing'. (This is of course wrong, since one who simply propounds a proposition may well do so for the purposes of, say, alarming his audience, or surprising it, or winning its approval; he may be warning, disclosing, pleading, or many other things.) It seems to have been supposed also, in the second place, and also wrongly, that, if one is (just, or perhaps even at all) stating or informing, then one's utterance cannot have any relevance to conduct, but only to 'belief'. (This is clearly wrong, since, if I inform you that some course of action is, say, highly dangerous, possibly meaning to do nothing *but* inform you of the fact, you have nevertheless in what I say a reason for not acting in that way, or at least for taking in doing so such care and precautions as you can.) Now, in consequence of these two errors, it was next supposed that, since in moral discourse the speaker is not always (just) stating or informing, and since what he says is typically highly relevant to conduct, old-school moral philosophers must be taken to have mis-identified, if only by implication, the 'use of language' which moral discourse actually involves. So philosophers were led to look round for some *other* 'use' of language – an 'emotive' use, or 'prescriptive' use, or what not – which could be offered as *the* use which moral discourse essentially exemplifies. But this is a wild goose chase. For just as what we may call propositional discourse does not involve any one particular 'use' of language – no one speaker's purpose, no one illocutionary force – so there is no particular 'use' of language in moral discourse; uses (in this sense) of language in moral discourse are enormously numerous, and just the *same*, for the most part, as in discourse that is not moral at all. In this way, old-school moral philosophers, instead of being reproved for the errors which (I dare say) they actually made, were charged with a mistake not implied by what they actually said – that of attributing only one, and that the wrong, 'use' of language to moral discourse; this mistake was in turn denounced for the wrong reasons; and this led to the emergence of entirely the wrong 'solution' – the idea that there is some *other* 'use' of language, definable in terms of its purpose or 'force', in moral discourse as such. That is a complicated paragraph, I fear; but the case is rather complicated.

In any case, I hope it may by now be reasonably clear why I said, at the beginning of this section, that there is really nothing special, or specially illuminating, about the *language* of moral discourse. The plain fact is that moral discourse, discourse on moral topics, just does not, as language, *differ* from discourse in general. It is not, of course – no one, so far as I know, has been so brazen as to suggest that it is – syntactically idiosyncratic. Though it probably has a few special items of vocabulary, most of the vocabulary of moral discourse is not peculiar to it. The purposes speakers may have in employing moral discourse, such as influencing, convincing, encouraging, deterring, and so on, are common to discourse on many other topics as well. And if we turn to Austinian illocutionary forces, we shall find that those instantiated in specimens of moral discourse are just the same as, and no less numerous than, those to be found in discourse in general. Thus it is not the language, or in any sense the 'use' of language, which distinguishes moral discourse from anything else. What is distinctive is the subject-matter, what the talk is about – specifically, the sorts of grounds that are stated or implied for the things that are said, the sorts of considerations that

к*

are taken to be relevant, and why. To study the language of morality is to study language, not morality; and even so, there is no
special interest in the language of *morality*. Or perhaps I should
say, no directly philosophical interest; it is doubtless interesting
historically, or etymologically, or sociologically, and thereby at
some points, perhaps, indirectly of some interest to philosophers
as well.

(C) MORALITY AND RELIGION

The question of the relations, both psychological and conceptual, between moral attitudes and religious beliefs is of course a
vast one, undoubtedly central to the history of morals, and also
of considerable philosophical complexity and interest. If I do
not offer very much about it here, the reason is not that I do not
recognize that to be so, but partly that I lack the required historical learning, and partly that I know my capacity for the
understanding of religious ideas to be very narrowly limited.
The main point I wish to make, which is not a profound one
though perhaps it has not always been recognized, is simply
that, when religious beliefs come into the picture, they must
inevitably change it very radically, make a very great difference;
and I shall try to say something of what sort of difference they
make, if only to establish that I am not wholly unaware of the
issues that arise here.

Of course, one must say at once that the proposition that
religious beliefs must make a very great difference is not unqualifiedly true; for religious beliefs differ in character, and some
may make very little difference if any. There have surely been
rather simple-minded, naïve forms of polytheism whose gods
were regarded, in effect, only as rather special, rather curious
members of the general population – able, no doubt, to do certain
extraordinary things like living for ever, appearing or dis-
appearing at will in this guise or that, controlling the winds and
the weather, and so on, but also ready to do quite ordinary
things like fighting in battles or seducing women, and equipped
on the whole with a fairly normal range of human qualities,
passions, propensities, even weaknesses and vices. A belief in
such gods might make little difference to one's moral ideas, if

one had any, just because they would not be regarded as very different from people. Then, at the other extreme, there have been religious beliefs whose god or gods have been so exceedingly *non*-human as scarcely to impinge upon human affairs at all. Aristotle, for instance, while he seems to have had the idea that there is a way in which some humans can, and, if they can, should become up to a point god-*like*, does not seem to me to think of his 'god' as *requiring* them to do this, or indeed as taking any interest whatever in what humans do; nor, incidentally, has his notion of being god-like any close connection with morality. If, however, for the present purpose we confine our attention to the more or less sophisticated species of monotheisms with which we are all more familiar – systems whose god is neither all-too-human nor just utterly non-human, and who is taken to be closely *concerned* with human doings – it can be seen, I think, that *such* beliefs must make a very great difference.

I shall mention first two sorts of difference which, though indeed great, can be regarded as in a sense incidental, not differences of principle. First, it is obvious, of course, that religious beliefs may make a very great difference simply to one's view of what one's situation actually is, of what the *facts* are. If I believe, for instance, that men have immortal souls, and that, if they act in certain ways, they are at any rate liable to suffer at God's hands the disagreeable fate of being eternally damned, then I will see, simply on the facts, a special, excellent reason why they should not act in those ways. Rather similarly, if persuaded that some course of action will lead to death and misery, perhaps for very many people, I may regard this, on the strength of my religious beliefs, as *in fact* not a specially important circumstance. For what is death, if souls are immortal? And what are a few months or years of terrestrial misery, compared with an eternity of bliss, or an eternity of torment? But this sort of difference need not be a difference of principle, or a difference of kind. If I hold that something should not be done because of the misery it will cause, and you hold that this misery would be merely a brief prelude to eternal rejoicing, then it may be only on the facts that we disagree; we reach a different conclusion, perhaps through applying just the *same* moral ideas to a case as to whose factual character we disagree. Similarly if I regard some act as entirely harmless, and you believe that, though terrestrially it may be, I shall be damned for doing it.

(Incidentally, it need not be regarded as very surprising that believers and non-believers do not in fact, all that often, come to grossly different practical conclusions. There is for one thing the point, of which too much is sometimes made (as perhaps by Nietzsche), that non-believers may, so to speak, uncritically inherit certain moral ideas from a tradition founded in beliefs which they no longer hold; and there is also the point that, in reasonably civilized societies, religious believers are not disposed to attribute to their deity requirements on conduct that seem too purely capricious, arbitrary, and pointless. It thus tends to come about, unsurprisingly enough, that the sanctions and rewards of religion are taken for the most part to be attached to conduct that would *anyway* be regarded as objectionable or the reverse, and at the same time that non-believers approve and disapprove what is believed by others to attract religious rewards and penalties. It is often stressed that religion influences moral ideas; it is equally obvious that moral ideas have influenced religions.)

Second, there is the point, which again I think is somewhat incidental, that religious belief *may* play an important part in instilling one of the essentials of 'the moral point of view'. It is an essential element in that point of view that – as a corollary of *general* concern with the human predicament – no human being is to be totally disregarded, to be seen as a thing without any right to be so much as considered, or to be used, like an animal or object, solely at another's will and pleasure. Now this idea may, of course, have a religious foundation. If I believe that all humans are alike in being 'sons of God', and that as such they figure in God's designs in a way to which inanimate nature and the brute creation cannot aspire, the moral significance, so to speak, of every human being may seem to me a wholly natural corollary. That this has been historically and conceptually important I would not, of course, question. Nevertheless it can be said, I believe, to be in a sense incidental. This is because the idea is itself, I think, really independent of religious belief. On the one hand, not all religious beliefs include it; some, even if their god is not overtly and exclusively tribal, seem to suppose him nevertheless to have favourites among humanity, so that by no means all humans can lay claim to equal consideration. Then, on the other hand, one may of course arrive at this idea without the prompting of religion; one may feel 'respect for persons' simply as *persons*, not necessarily as items under the special care of a deity. I suspect that some religious believers might maintain that, though this may be so, the moral idea of the (in some sense) equality of mankind as such does not really *make sense* outside a religious context; but I doubt very much whether this claim could really be substantiated without recourse to some criterion of what it is to 'make sense' according to which it would not really make sense in religious terms either.

What, then, is it that makes the genuine difference of principle? I believe, though with considerable diffidence, that the answer is this: religious belief (of the kind we are considering) brings on to the stage, so to speak, an element that has absolutely no parallel, to which nothing is at all comparable, among the infidel's *dramatis personae* – namely, a being to which, in a quite unique sense, veneration is owed, which is uniquely an object of both love and fear, and above all to whose behests is owed, uniquely, *obedience*. This is not just, as has often been suggested, a question of believing something to be the case which the infidel supposes not to be the case in fact; it is taking something to be the case which inevitably transforms the whole picture. For where it is supposed that God has spoken on some matter of conduct, then deliberately to act wrongly must be seen as objectionable not merely on any grounds that an infidel might share, nor merely on account of any supposed supernatural consequences; the act has, in a way to which the infidel can find no parallel, the peculiar character of disobedience, of wilful disrespect, shown towards overwhelming authority, and overwhelming power. This introduces, of course, an absolute difference of principle between those questions of conduct on which respectively it is supposed that God has, and has not, pronounced. It is possible for the believer to come to regard acting wrongly or badly (or, for that matter, rightly and well) in some purely 'human' respect as comparatively a trivial matter; but above all, whether trivial or not, it is quite different in kind. For no purely 'human', 'natural' disasters, follies, or even crimes have that character of cosmic disobedience, disrespect to God. Thus, the believer can, even must, regard *some* questions of conduct as sharply and totally distinct in character from others, where the infidel may see rather, perhaps, a penumbral gradation; and he may, even must, regard some requirements on conduct as having a unique, overwhelming importance, a quite peculiar authority, in a way to which infidel ethics can offer no analogy. Some may wish to say here that this exposes the impossibility of an infidel ethics; for some would say that, if one does *not* find in certain questions of conduct this sort of uniqueness, of unique importance and weight, then one has missed seeing *morality* entirely, one is simply blind to it; one has allowed its proper place to be taken in one's mind by something else altogether, perhaps some kind of higher expediency or generalized prudence. Well, one could of course make that true by definition; one could make it, in effect, true by definition that purely secular, 'natural' considerations cannot issue in anything of genuinely *moral* significance. However, I see no reason why such a definition of the subject should be accepted – which is to say that I do not believe, any more than Kant did, that 'moral consciousness' must necessarily be allied with religious belief. But nor do I believe, as I think Kant fundamentally did, that one can make good sense in purely secular terms of the *same kind* of moral consciousness as the religious believer may have. If there is no authority, then there really are no Imperatives; it is true that, if there is no God, then everything is 'permitted' – not of course in the sense that nothing is morally either right or wrong, but in the sense that nothing is *commanded*, and nothing *forbidden*. It is not reasonable to deny that there is, and of course it is not surprising that there should be, a use of the term 'moral' that is accessible and intelligible to unbelievers; but it cannot, in my view, be anything like the *same* use as that use which the term can have in a religious context. If one is to construct a 'theory' of morals, it must be made clear in advance whether religious beliefs are therein presupposed or not; for, accordingly as they are or are not, it will be a different phenomenon that one's theory will be called upon to grapple with.

9. Morals and Rationality

To whom do the principles of morality apply? In this final chapter I want to consider this decidedly unclear question, and some important further issues which, I think, quite naturally arise from answers to it.

In one way of construing the question, an answer to it has already been sketched very briefly at an earlier stage.[1] If one asks to whom the law of, say, France applies, one good way, I suppose, of understanding the question would be to take it as asking who is liable under French law, or who can properly be required to comply with its provisions; similarly, in asking to whom moral principles apply, the question may be who is liable to be morally 'judged' (in this case, of course, either by himself or others), or who can properly be required in some sense to comply with moral principles. The unsurprising answer to this question that was briefly suggested earlier was: rational beings. And I think we can now see fairly easily that, and why, and in what sense this answer is correct.

Moral principles, as we have seen, generate a certain range of reasons – moral reasons – for and against actions and courses of action. To act morally well – which is not quite the same thing as to act morally creditably, though perhaps the distinction is not crucial here – is to accord to such reasons, where of course there are any, their due weight in deciding on one's courses of action, and to act appropriately to such decisions; to act morally badly is to fail to do this. If so, it is clearly a necessary condition of being judged to have acted either morally well or morally badly that one should be *capable* of doing that, or of failing to; for we do not 'require' a person to do, or hold him responsible for not doing, what he is not capable of doing, just as, I suppose, we would not regard him as either commendable or blameworthy for

[1] In chapter 2.

doing something which in fact he could not *not* have done. That is to say, then, that to be a 'moral agent', the kind of creature capable of acting morally well or ill, and therefore liable to moral judgement in the light of his actions, is, as a necessary condition, to be a rational being in just this rather limited sense – namely, that one is able to achieve some understanding of the situations in which one may be placed, to envisage alternative courses of action in those situations, to grasp and weigh considerations for or against those alternatives, and to act accordingly. What is required are certain capacities of understanding and thought, a certain capacity of choice, and also, of course, if these capacities are actually to be exercised, alternative courses of action, at least sometimes, between which to choose. It will be obvious that rationality, even in this rather limited sense, is a matter of degree, and also that it may be absent, or imperfectly present, in principle at any rate in two different ways; one may, for one reason or another, be unable or inadequately able to understand and think, or – perhaps a less commonly recognized possibility – one may be unable or not fully able to choose and to act in accordance with one's thoughts. Compulsive acts, I take it, are acts which the agent is not able or not fully able not to do, even if he is perfectly well able to understand what those acts are, and what reasons there may be for not acting in that way.

Rationality, then, we may say, in this limited sense is a necessary condition of the applicability to one's doings of moral principles – this being really just a particular instance of the general principle that one is 'required' to do only what, in at any rate some degree, one is able to do. But is it also a sufficient condition? I suggested earlier that it was not – but, one may think, in a rather uninteresting way. I suggested, namely, that it is not inconceivable that there should be rational beings for whom, so to speak, the whole question would not arise – either because, in the circumstances in which they were placed, there just never were any moral reasons for or against any of the courses of action open to them, or perhaps – a less clear possibility – because in some way they just naturally, as it were automatically, did what was morally proper, being in some sense or other unable to do, perhaps seriously to contemplate doing, anything else.

(Perhaps they have no 'inclinations', in Kant's sense, which would ever conflict with their perception of moral reasons.) But this is perhaps not very interesting, if only for the reason that, obviously enough, it involves the fancying of conditions which, for most and perhaps all rational beings, do not and could not possibly obtain in fact. So what about rational beings in their actual predicament? Could it ever be said of such a being, so placed, that, though he satisfied the necessary conditions for the applicability of moral principles, nevertheless for some reason they did not actually apply to him?

I believe that the answer to this question must be that it could not. One might think at first sight that to say this was excessively severe. Are we, one might protest, to apply the full rigour of moral principles – 'our' moral principles – to humans who, though rational in the sense of being able in some degree to understand, deliberate, and decide, yet live, for instance, in such a state of civilization or want of it as not reasonably to be expected ever to have formed any moral ideas at all? It is, after all, a presupposition of our own way of proceeding that members of some societies, and perhaps some members of all societies, can be said to have, no doubt for perfectly understandable reasons, no moral concepts; and if so, how can moral principles 'apply' to them? But this protest is confused. It confuses, I think, the question of the applicability of moral principles with the question of the justifiability of moral blame. A man may quite properly be judged to have acted criminally, even though it might have been unreasonable to expect him to act otherwise. If, for instance, he were born and brought up in a family and community of habitual criminals, we might think that he was not much to be blamed for taking to a life of crime, and, when he falls foul of the law, we might urge his unfortunate background and history in mitigation of punishment – how could such a person be reasonably expected to feel any respect for the law? Still, if of sound mind, he will be nevertheless one of those to whom the law applies, and whose voluntary acts accordingly, whether blameworthy or not, can certainly be said to be criminal. Somewhat similarly, there is nothing, I think, to debar us from saying that, say, some medieval Scottish chieftain acted morally badly in slaughtering all the rival clansmen whom he had invited to a banquet, even though we might well think it right to go on to say that such a person, of course, is scarcely to be blamed for so acting – he was merely conforming, and quite naturally so, with the accepted *mores* of upper-class Scottish life of the period. It might be objected that there is an important difference here; our criminal presumably knows that his acts are criminal – though he has no respect for law, he knows what law is, and is perhaps more familiar than most with its detailed provisions; but the Scottish chieftain does not, surely, know what morality is, and may be violating no principles of whose force he is at all aware. But there is not much in this. The condition of criminal liability, in fact, is not so much that one does know the law, as that one could (and should); somewhat similarly, I think, to be said to have acted morally badly, it is not necessary that one should have seen one's act as in breach of moral principle, nor even that one could have been reasonably expected to do so, but only that one should have been capable of doing so – should have had the sort of capacities that make such realization possible. But those the Scottish chieftain presumably had, however vain might have been the hope that he would actually exercise them in the way that morality would enjoin. If so, he is one of those to whom moral principles 'apply', however little we may think it proper to blame him for acting in gross conflict with those principles. Not all offenders who are criminally liable are regarded, or should be regarded, as equally culpable. There may be many to whose actions moral principles apply who are not blameworthy at all for acting morally badly.

We need not say, then, that moral principles do not apply to rational beings who, in their own thoughts about their own or others' conduct, do not, and perhaps could not be expected to, advert to any moral considerations. Is there any other ground on which exemption, so to speak, from morality might be claimed? For my part I do not see how there possibly could be; for what could be relevantly urged in support of such a claim? The case is different with, say, rules of law, or rules of institutions such as, let us say, a university. Rules of law after all (if we may ignore here the tricky and disputable case of international law) overtly do not aspire to any quite *general* regulation of behaviour; emanating as they typically do from national authority, their concern is with, and they apply to, their own nationals, or perhaps it would be better to say, those transacting affairs in that national territory. (I am sure the position is really more complicated than that, but not in a way that matters here.) Similarly a university's rules aim at regulating the doings of members of that university. Thus in each case there is an obvious way in which exemption can be claimed – one is not of the right nationality or not in the right place, one is not a member of the institution concerned. But we have suggested here that the 'object' of morality is a perfectly general amelioration, or non-deterioration, of the human predicament; and that surely is something from which no human can be seen, or could in any way claim, to be excluded. Here there is surely no such thing as 'not being a member'. Let us not get confused here. I am not attempting to maintain that everything that could be called a moral principle applies to everybody; for there are of course, derivatively for instance from the general principle of obligation, particular principles as to what, say, parents should do, or married persons should not do, and these will of course apply only to parents and married persons, probably, indeed, only to parents and married persons in particular societies or social circumstances. The basic principles of morality, however, mention no such special status as that of a parent or a spouse; they mention humans – indeed, less restrictedly even than that in principle, rational beings. Again, it is certainly no part of my suggestion that moral principles apply *always*; I see no reason to question the natural supposition that sometimes morality does not apply for the reason that, in some instances, there is in the circumstances nothing of any moral relevance; nor would I wish to exclude the further possibility that, perhaps in very desperate and extreme and abnormal circumstances, one might regard as suspended moral considerations which, in more ordinary circumstances, would certainly be relevantly applicable. If it is true that *inter arma silent leges*, it is at any rate arguable that morality too may be dumb in some extreme situations. My suggestion is only that, if the object of morality is a *general* amelioration of the predicament of rational beings, a rational being could not claim to be *in general* not the kind of agent to whose doings the principles of morality could be held applicable; and hence that to be rational in the weakish sense outlined above is, for the applicability of those principles to one's doings, a sufficient condition as well as a necessary one. And we are not, I hope, making an unnecessary fuss about this. It might be said, I think rightly, to be an analytic proposition that the principles of morality apply to 'everybody', all rational beings; but in this case, as in others, it is scarcely sufficient (for philosophical purposes) just to assert, however truly, that the proposition is analytic. For after we have said what some concept analytically contains, there arises, unless indeed the concept is a more or less arbitrary construct, the question why the concept *should* be such as analytically to contain that. In this case, if we ask why the concept of morality should be such as to make it analytic that its principles apply to 'everybody', we have to turn, as so often in my view, for illumination to some consideration of what the apparatus of morality is for.

Let us now consider the question to whom the principles of morality apply from, so to speak, the other end – from the standpoint not of the agent, but of the 'patient'. What, we may ask here, is the condition of moral *relevance*? What is the condition of having a claim to be *considered*, by rational agents to whom moral principles apply?

Well, first of all, it is important here, though also in my opinion fairly easy, to rule out what might be called 'closed', or 'tribal' moralities. There have existed from time to time, and doubtless do exist, many curious instances of codes – often spoken of by anthropologists and others as moral codes – taken by their devotees to be of more or less sharply restricted applicability. Such a code may, for instance, require me to give aid to, or strictly abstain from violence towards, other members of my tribe, or my feudal rank, or my class, or whatever it may be, while subjecting me to no such, or perhaps not even to any, requirements in my relations with non-members of that group. Thus there have been persons for whom, while it would be thought a very terrible thing deliberately to injure a fellow-tribes-man, there was felt to be no objection at all to robbing with violence the occasional foreigner, and perhaps even great merit in killing him for the sake of his scalp; there have been white men who, loyal and considerate and so on towards other white men, have seemed to recognize no such claim to consideration of other persons who happen not to be white. Such codes, as I have said, are often spoken of as moral codes; it would be orthodox usage enough to remark that 'the morality' of, say, the head-hunting tribesman regulates his dealings only with fellow-members of the tribe, and does not apply to his relations with any other persons. Such talk can be readily understood, and so far is no doubt unobjectionable; but I believe that it can also be said, with both point and truth, that such a code, while indeed it can be called *a* morality, is not morality – to see things so is not to see them from the moral point of view, and such notions, while wholly understandable, are not moral notions. But if to say this is not to be just arbitrary, what justifies one in saying it? Well, one can at least begin, in my view, by saying that it is *analytic* that principles of morality are not thus circumscribed in their application; it is part of the concept – the 'special' concept if you like – of morality that no person is simply excluded from moral consideration, and furthermore – as perhaps scarcely needs to be separately mentioned – that if he is to be considered differently from some other person, the difference made must be justified by some morally relevant ground of distinction. (What is morally 'relevant' follows, of course, from what morality is; it is not an arbitrary matter, or a matter of choice or opinion.) However, though one can begin, in my view absolutely rightly, by saying that all this is analytic, as before one must go on to say something as to why it should be; and we turn here, as before, to consider what morality is for.

The point is a simple one really. The general object of the exercise is, in a predicament in which things are liable to go badly for people (not here morally badly, just *badly*), to countervail in a certain way their liability to do so; and in particular, to do so by mitigating in some degree the ill effects that are inherently liable to flow from the *indifference* of persons to other persons, or even positive hostility. Now it is clear that a system of principles evolved to this end will not actually achieve that end, or not achieve it fully, if the scope of such principles is thought of as confined within groups. For two reasons. First, everyone presumably will be a non-member of some group, and cannot in general have any absolute guarantee that he will encounter no members of groups that are not his own; thus, if principles are group-bound, he remains, so to speak, at risk – at diminished risk, possibly, but still he will be liable to encounter persons whose natural indifference or hostility towards him will be countervailed by no principles of which they see him as a potential beneficiary. Second, and probably more seriously, if conduct is to be seen as regulated only *within* groups, we have still the possibility of unrestricted hostility and conflict *between* groups – which is liable, indeed, to be effectively ferocious and damaging exactly in proportion as relations between individuals within each group are effectively ordered towards harmonious co-operative action. Thus, just as one may think that a Hobbesian recipe for 'peace' could securely achieve its end only if all Hobbesian individuals were engrossed within a *single* irresistible Leviathan, there is reason to think that the principles of morality must, if the object of morality is not to be frustrated, give consideration to *any* human, of whatever special groups or none he may in fact be a member. It is for this reason, I think, that the concept of morality is such – and, given what morality is for, *has* to be such – that it is analytic that moral principles are, as it were from the receiving end, not restricted in their scope. This seems to me to be the point, and the *rationale* of the point, in the widely-felt idea that the essence of morality is 'respect for persons', and perhaps also in the idea that there are 'natural' rights, independent of status or any special claims.

But there is more to be said. Moral *agents*, we have said, are rational beings; if we now say that the beneficiaries, so to speak, of moral principles are, unrestrictedly, persons, should we take 'person' here to mean 'rational being'? There is plain reason, I believe, to hold that we should not so take it – to hold, indeed, that 'person' is itself too restrictive a term here. Notice, first, that we do not in fact place this limitation upon the class of beneficiaries of moral principle. We do not regard infants and imbeciles as moral agents, as liable to judgement for their conduct on moral principles, since we take them not to possess those rational capacities which are a condition of being capable of moral thought and decision; but we do not for that reason regard them as morally insignificant, as having, that is, no moral *claims* upon rational beings. Why is this? Is it that they are in some sense, though not actual, yet potential rational beings, members, so to speak, of a potentially rational species? I do not think so. Infants no doubt could be said to be potentially rational; but is it for that reason that they are not to be, say, physically maltreated? Not all imbeciles, I dare say, *are* potentially rational; but does it follow that, if they are reasonably judged to be incurable, they are then reasonably to be taken to have no moral claims? No: the basis of moral claims seems to me to be quite different. We may put it thus: just as liability to be judged as a moral agent follows from one's general capability of alleviating, by moral action, the ills of the predicament, and is for that reason confined to rational beings, so the condition of being a proper 'beneficiary' of moral action is the capability of *suffering* the ills of the predicament – and for that reason is *not* confined to rational beings, nor even to potential members of that class. Things go badly, in general, if creatures suffer, better if they do not; to come within the ambit, then, of the ameliorative object of moral principles is, not to be capable of contributing to such amelioration, but to be capable of suffering by its absence – that is, capable of suffering. But if so, the class, if one may put it so, of moral patients may be thought to be wider even than the class of 'persons'; for there is ample reason to think – though indeed attempts have at times been made to think otherwise – that animals can suffer. How far down the scale, so to speak, of the brute creation should moral relevance be taken to extend? There is perhaps reason to say, without directly answering that question, that it extends just as far as does the capacity to suffer – though in practice we seem to be conscious of moral claims in non-humans in some sort of proportion, partly to the degree of their actual involvement (as with domestic animals and pets) in human communities, and partly perhaps to the degree to which they are, crudely, 'like us' – mammals in this way outranking birds and fishes, snakes and insects scarcely counting at all. But no doubt natural feelings on such a point are often largely irrational; and certainly they seem to differ pretty widely from one person to another. We need not, I think, fortunately, here try to adjudicate.

I turn now to an issue of considerably greater complexity. We have argued so far that it is part of the *concept* of morality – and understandably so in the light of what morality is for – that the principles of morality apply to (as agents) all rational beings, and to (as patients) all creatures capable of suffering. I want now to ask whether there is any sense, and if so what sense, in which any rational being *must*, so far as rational, 'accept' moral principles, or recognize and apply them in his practical judgement and practice. We recognize, but here ignore, the case of one who, like the medieval Scottish chieftain, has never 'got the idea' of morality; we are to consider the case of one who, while he has the idea, in some sense does not 'accept' it. Could such a rational being, so to speak, just *reject* morality, without necessarily evidencing thereby any defect of rationality? Very many moral philosophers, perhaps most conspicuously Kant, have wished to hold that the answer to that question must be No: I am inclined to disagree with them; but the issue is not a simple one, and will take a little sorting out.

Let us take notice, first, of one relatively uncontroversial possibility. It is fairly obviously possible, without manifest defect of rationality, to 'reject' morality by denying what might be called its psychological basis – as even Kant, I imagine, might have been brought to agree. What I have in mind is this. Morality, as here depicted, is a system of (fundamental, and thence of course derivative) principles which, in application to the circumstances of particular cases, generate a certain range of reasons for and against the doing of things; and the system, to speak loosely but intelligibly, is supposed to 'work' by way of the emergence in rational beings of dispositions (virtues) disinterestedly and without coercion to give due weight to such reasons in appraising actions, whether their own or of other people. Now it would surely be not irrational, though it may be in fact mistaken, to hold that this is not really psychologically possible – that a system that is meant to work in this way presupposes that people can do (since it calls on them to do it) what they are not really able to do, and never do in fact. There is more than one way in which this position might be argued for. Most familiarly perhaps, though far from most clearly, one might hold that morality pre-supposes 'the freedom of the will', in some sense in which actually there is reason to think the will not free. Quite famili-arly again, one might argue that people are really, inherently, immutably, and exclusively self-interested, and so simply not capable of that disinterested appraisal of reasons, that unegoistic concern for others, which morality professes to desiderate. Or again, rather differently, and in more briskly up-to-date terms, one might hold that the real determinants of action and of practical judgement are not reasons at all, not even self-interested reasons, but psychological needs and 'drives' perhaps partly or even wholly below the threshold of conscious recognition. These are issues, it seems clear, not to be wholly settled, though no doubt they might be valuably clarified, by philosophical argu-ment; it is a question of fact, after all, what people are capable of, or are capable of becoming capable of. Let us be content, then, here with taking note of the general fact that morality, because of the way it is supposed to 'work', does have psychological pre-suppositions; quite obviously, in requiring that the judgement and conduct of rational beings should be guided, where rele-vant, by appraisal of a certain range of un-self-interested reasons, one presupposes that this is *possible*; and the 'system' may be re-jected on the ground of flat denial that it is. (Compare with this certain criticisms of traditional systems of law as psychologically unrealistic, and particularly of traditional concepts of legal re-sponsibility and punishment.) At the most, if one takes the pre-supposed psychological basis to be unsound, one might give qualified acceptance to morality as something other than it superficially professes to be – perhaps as a harmless but ineffi-cacious illusion, or even (as perhaps some emotivists actually have done) as a mode of actual psychological expression and interaction between persons merely posing as, and by some naïve-ly taken as, a system of reasoning. One might even think (as some Utilitarians, for rather different reasons, have done) that the system owes such practical efficacy as it has precisely to *mis*-understanding of its actual character; even if, in 'arguing' with you, I am really just psychologically pushing and pulling, my propensity to push and pull, and to do so with effect, may depend on my, or your, belief that that is *not* what I am doing. In any case, since the truth of psychological propositions about people is always an issue of fact and often an issue of quite legitimate controversy, I take it that it is clearly not *irrational*, though it may be mistaken, to 'reject' morality in this sort of way, as unworkable.

Next, there is nothing, it seems to me, in the least *irrational* in the idea that morality should be rejected as somehow a fraud. It will be easy to see this if we start from a partial analogy, from some system of rules. Consider the case of, say, a university community, in which various rules and regulations are in force with respect to the conduct of its members; and let us make further the supposition, at one time not unplausible, that, while these rules and regulations apply to all members of the community, they are formulated, promulgated, and enforced by only some of them; in this matter 'senior' members exercise authority and power over 'junior' ones. Now it might well be the official view of these various prescriptions that their observance was for the good of the community at large; there are, it might be held, certain standards and procedures proper to, perhaps essential to, the good conduct of the life of an academic body, and since all members of the community will benefit if their corporate academic affairs are well rather than ill conducted, it is from everyone's point of view a good thing that rules directed to this good end should be made and faithfully observed, and, if necessary, enforced. Such might well be the official view; and if so, it is not at all difficult to see how it might be maintained that 'the system' was really a fraud. There are in fact several possibilities here. It might be suggested, simply and directly, that general observance of the rules was really beneficial only to those who made them, and that they were made for that reason – what the rules do, and are intended to do, is to keep the majority docile, silent, untroublesome, and powerless, so that the senior oligarchy can peacefully pursue its private ends without exertion or the need to justify what it is about. Or it might be maintained, slightly more charitably, that the authorities are not so much consciously dishonest as self-deluded – that their official justification of the system is sincere in a way, but only because they have repressed all capacity to distinguish the good of the community at large from what suits themselves. Or again, deeper thinkers among dissenters might take the line that the authorities themselves are also victims in a broader context – that they are, perhaps quite unwittingly, responding to the pressures of society outside the university altogether, and regulating the conduct of its affairs really in the interests, not even of themselves, but of the power structure, politicians, the military-industrial complex, or some other very villainous entity of that sort. In any case, in some such way it might well be argued that the official, *bienpensant* view of the system of rules was at variance, perhaps wittingly and dishonestly so, with the reality of the case – the system is officially advertised, justified, or 'sold' as tending towards some generally acceptable good end, whereas in fact, and perhaps by design, it promotes another one.

If we turn back now to the more general case of morality, we can distinguish, I think, at least two variants of this form of argument; let us call them the Marxist and the Thrasymachean, without insisting on the strict historical aptness of these labels. What I have in mind as a Marxist variant would be the contention that, while there certainly are fundamental moral principles, of justice and charity and so on, yet the applications, specifications, or concrete realizations of these in any actual society are, perhaps not deliberately but inevitably, always distorted – distorted, namely, in such a way as to advance the interests of the 'class' which happens historically to be dominant in that society. There is in principle such a thing, for example, in any society as justice in the distribution of rewards for labour, but in fact, in any society which is not classless, what is generally, as it were officially, *said* to be just, and commended as just, in that matter is not just really, but biassed in the interests of the dominant class. And thus there would arise an accepted, generally propagated, 'official' moral outlook which was really fraudulent – supposed to be generally, impersonally good for everyone alike, while it is in fact good only for some, for its official propagandists. What I call the Thrasymachean line would be more radical than this: it would be the contention that all moral concepts are intrinsically hollow – that what, for example, is officially regarded as 'just' is not merely a distortion of what in some sense is really just, but is a mere mask concealing a wholly amoral reality. What actually goes on, it might be held on this view, is simply that men pursue, more or less clear-sightedly, interests of their own; but some, if they can, contrive to further their own ends by foisting upon others the idea that those others 'ought' and 'ought not' to do certain things, thereby inducing them, if they are gullible enough, sometimes to sacrifice their own advantage to the interests of those by whom they are thus manipulated. Nothing really *is* 'morally' right or wrong; in reality there are only personal interests, more or less clearsightedly, tenaciously, and successfully pursued. 'Morality' is a kind of smoke-screen concealing this stern reality from some, and inducing them more readily to submit in sheeplike docility to the exploitation of others.

Either of these lines, it seems to me, could be taken quite understandably, however mistakenly, by a rational man. What I have called the Marxist view is in fact scarcely more than an exaggeration of a point that is perfectly familiar and unsurprising – namely, that both individuals and groups are somewhat prone to consider, quite sincerely if self-deceivingly, as requirements of morality what suits themselves. To base on this a *general* indictment of morality is merely to insist, intelligibly though admittedly with the highest implausibility, that in fact this occurs not merely sometimes, but always. Such an indictment, it should be noted, is merely factually, not conceptually, revolutionary or radical. It is not the principles and concepts of morality themselves that are attacked, or anyway not in general, but only the specific moral conclusions that are generally, conventionally accepted in particular societies. It is at this point that the Thrasymachean seeks to go further; he seeks to reject morality *itself*, and not merely particular conventions and 'official' views. But perhaps there is a certain ambiguity in this enterprise, to resolve which will lead us on to further possibilities. It might be the idea that, while, as a matter of purely idle speculation, one could conceive of principles general observance of which would be for the general good, yet a system of such principles should be condemned as completely 'unreal' for the reason that in fact it is simply not going to be adopted; without necessarily maintaining that its adoption would be a psychological impossibility, one might yet claim that its non-adoption was a practical certainty, and hence that the 'realist' should face the practical conclusion that he finds himself in fact in a world of competitive egoists, and ought not to compete there under the restrictions that morality would entail – for in practice, if not in speculative principle, to accept such restrictions would merely leave him a prey to the predatory designs of others. Rather different from this is the idea – to which we shall return – that morality is to be rejected on the ground that the object it professes, even if it were achievable and achieved, would not be a good thing.

It is not irrational, then, though it may be in fact mistaken, to hold that morality is not psychologically practicable; nor is it irrational, though again it may be in fact mistaken, to hold that morality is, as things are, a sort of fraud. There is the further and very different possibility, it seems to me, of holding that morality is not particularly *important*. I do not mean merely that it is possible rationally to hold that, say, breaches of moral principle are not *necessarily* important; for this, I should assume, we are nearly all disposed to think anyway. It is a very common view, I should think, and not a manifestly wrong one, that while, say, moral offences are often very serious matters, and it is often a matter of great importance that what is morally right should be done, yet there is also a class of pretty harmless moral peccadilloes – small untruths, for example, told with no harmful consequences, for vanity's sake, or to avoid embarrassment – which, while undoubted instances of moral obliquity, are of negligible importance. It might be properly urged here, indeed, that, rather as it is doubtless of importance for law and order that people in general should be disposed not to commit even minor, fairly trivial crimes, so it may be of importance from the moral point of view that people should be disposed to abstain even from harmless, minor moral obliquity; even so, unless one sees moral wrong-doing as an offence to a Creator, or in some other way as *intrinsically* of vast importance, it would seem to me difficult to resist the conclusion that at least some moral wrongs really do not matter very much. But what I have in mind here is not this unexciting conclusion; I have in mind the idea, which seems rationally perfectly tenable, that moral reasons as such, being *among* considerations relevant to practical issues, and accordingly liable to be weighed in the balance against others, may, when so weighed, be adjudged not decisively weighty. If I own, say, a beautiful and historic building which, in the interests of those obliged to live in the locality, ought to be demolished, is it *irrational* to think that the moral claims of those people do not necessarily outweigh the undesirability of destroying a beautiful and historic building? If I believe that I am capable of composing, say, magnificent music, is it irrational to think that I should, if necessary, neglect my obligations to my dependent wife, children, and aged parents in order to do so? I might, of course, in such cases believe myself *morally* justified; I might hold that my building, or my music, constituted a contribution to the well-being of persons, possibly of posterity, which *morally* outweighed the moral claims of those more immediately detrimentally affected. But I think I need not do so. It seems to me possible to see in, say, aesthetic objects a value for themselves, not merely for their place in the lives of people in general, which, if so, may sometimes be weighed *against* moral values, and by some may sometimes be regarded as of greater weight.

It is not possible to doubt, I believe, that such a 'placing' of morality – some such subordination of the weight of moral reasons to others – does sometimes occur; and, though possibly there may be some way of arguing that such down-grading, so to speak, of moral considerations is 'contrary to reason', I cannot for my own part see how such an argument would go. It has, of course, certainly been held by some to be *analytic* that, where moral considerations are applicable, they preponderate over considerations of any other sort, and hence that to take any considerations whatever to be 'more important' than moral ones is really a contradiction. But how is this allegation to be explained or defended? One might say that moral considerations, for any person, are just those considerations which *are* in practice, for him, preponderant over any others; that, however, has the obviously unacceptable consequence that everyone necessarily, however bizarre his principles and practice may be, must be said to be regularly guided by moral principles. But if one does not thus, as it were, build predominant importance directly into one's definition of moral considerations, from what constituent *in* that definition is their predominant importance to be, inexorably, extracted? One could do the trick again, no doubt, with the help of a deity; but, without recourse to that, I do not myself see how to hold that a rational being could not suppose that, while moral reasons certainly were reasons, there might sometimes be *other* reasons by which they were outweighed. Such a view very often, no doubt, *is* taken irrationally. If, for instance, I hold that the interests of my country should always over-ride, where necessary, moral considerations, I may well be in the genuinely irrational position of maintaining that the interests of some persons constitute good reason for acting and of others not, while being unable to produce any relevant difference whatever in support of this distinction. But what if I value beauty, say, more highly than justice? 'Creativity', or some such thing, more highly than moral conscientiousness? I do not see that reason rules decisively against such valuations.

Next, is it possible to hold, without gross defect of reason, that morality is actually a *bad thing*? To hold, that is, not merely that moral reasons may sometimes be outweighed by other, better reasons, but that they are never really *good* reasons at all? I believe, perhaps depressingly, that it is indeed quite possible to hold this. One might hold, for instance, either that the 'object' of morality is one which it would not be a good thing to achieve, or possibly that the 'moral' way is not the way to achieve it. There may be other possibilities also, but let us briefly consider these two.

One might advert, first, to an absolutely basic supposition on which our picture of morality has been constructed – the supposition, namely, that that in the human predicament which it is the 'object', or point, of morality to countervail is *bad*. Our notion has been that, given the inherent limitation of human sympathies, there would be reason to anticipate that, if people acted as they were 'just naturally' disposed to do, those vulnerable to aggression might expect to be victims of it; those in need of help might find that no help was forthcoming; those without special claims to favour might suffer discrimination; that one man should trust another might be simply unreasonable; and so on. Earlier, of course, we assumed that this would be a bad thing – partly because, we supposed, it would render impossible much, and particularly much co-operative enterprise, for which the need is clear, and partly because of the direct deprivations and sufferings that, in our 'state of nature', would be surely unavoidable. We have insisted, of course, that we are not here begging any *moral* questions; deprivations and sufferings were not taken to be *morally* bad, just as Hobbes's 'state of nature', though bad indeed – 'nasty' – was not morally bad. But – it is possible to ask – is this *bad* at all? If the vulnerable suffer from aggression, the strong aggressor does not; if no help is forthcoming, success goes to those strong enough, resourceful enough, to succeed without help; 'injustice' denies goods to those with no 'natural' claim to them. Why, it may be asked, should the weak and undistinguished, the helpless and dependent, be protected from the natural consequences of their contemptible condition? Why should the formidable and strong, the self-sufficient and intelligent, be denied the full fruits of their natural advantages? No one, surely, *admires* the condition of feebleness and dependence; everyone, including the feeble, sees clearly that it is *better* to be strong and active, self-reliant and able; winners are preferable to losers, masters to slaves – even slaves and losers think so. But if so, why is it better, by a sort of mean conspiracy of the naturally under-endowed, to shackle the strong in the exercise of their admirable strength, and to prop up all those palsied nonentities who cannot stand on their own? Left to itself, so to speak, what is naturally admirable will naturally flourish; what is naturally despised and despicable will be duly abased. And what is bad about that? It is as if, in morality, there were incorporated a kind of question-begging egalitarian democracy; we have mentioned already the idea of 'respect for persons' – but what is there, after all, in most persons that merits respect? Or what in their 'nature' confers any rights upon them? Why struggle against the obvious truth that men are *not* equal, and that those who cannot survive therein show themselves unfit to do so? But if we think thus we shall reject the whole *object* of morality; we shall not think it a good thing, even if it were practically achievable, to restrict by moral principles what the naturally strong may do, or to set limits by moral principles to what the weak may suffer. It is not necessary to deny here that sufferings and deprivations, even death, are in themselves bad things; for one may think, in somewhat Nietzschean style, that nonetheless it is *right* that such bad things should accrue to those unable to defend themselves against them, and correspondingly *wrong* to restrain the heroic energies of those naturally able to secure good things for themselves. It is thus possible, in a sense, both to see what morality does, and to see also, at least up to a point, for what reason it is done, and yet to hold, quite in general, that that is a *wrong* thing to do.

Secondly, one may mention here the less familiar idea that, even if the 'object' of morality were conceded to be good, one might regard as objectionable its route, so to speak, to that object. Morality, it might be said, as we have depicted it here, involves essentially *inhibition* of the natural inclinations of human beings; we have argued indeed that there is a place, or case, for morality precisely because people are *not* just naturally disposed to act in the way that is morally right. Now this, it could possibly be argued, would be all very well if it were possible to believe, as for instance Aristotle did, in the feasibility of actually modifying the nature of persons – of bringing it about, that is, by suitable training and education that they should genuinely cease to have those natural inclinations that run counter to the requirements of morality, but instead become naturally disposed to act, and to take pleasure in acting, as morality requires. But this, it might be held, is in fact not possible at all; the fact is that one must recognize, with Kant and Freud and most if not all kinds of Christians, that inclinations to act morally wrongly are quite ineradicable in human beings – they can at best be controlled, not got rid of, repressed, not annihilated. But the consequence of that might be said to be that morality can 'work', as we put it earlier, only at the cost of continuous psychological damage – damage consisting partly in the unhappiness and anxiety of conscious conflict, and partly, probably much more seriously, in the consequences, below the conscious threshold, of severe repression. It is less clear, I think, when one has said this, what one says next. It would be possible, I take it, to adopt the merely fatalistic conclusion that the object of morality is simply not attainable at all – there is only a choice between the obvious, overt disagreeablenesses of a more or less Hobbesian state of nature, and the less manifest miseries of a general psychic *malaise* intensifying, perhaps, in quite direct proportion to the success of mankind in achieving so-called 'civilization'. But I suppose one might hopefully hypothesize some yet-to-be-excogitated means of countering the inherent ills of the human predicament, without incurring the alleged psychological costs of what we now call 'morality'.

I believe that, depressing to some though this conclusion may be, neither of the positions thus crudely sketched can be said to be irrational. The latter, indeed, turns primarily upon a question of fact (though no doubt not of 'hard' fact): is it the case, that is, that the price of morality, in terms of unavoidable psychological conflict and repression, is actually so high as to cancel, or make nugatory, the hoped-for dividends of peace, of justice, of co-operative harmony? Is it true that our choice lies only between roughly comparable evils? One may think that this question is in fact not all that hard to answer; for though civilized man, no doubt, is liable to be a distressing spectacle of neuroses, anxieties and general psychological disarray, it is not easy to believe that things would not be considerably *worse* if the constraints of morality were universally dissolved. The opposite view, however, though perhaps contrary to good sense, is not contrary to reason. Nor, I think, can it be said that the former position – that of, we may tendentiously call it, the Free Enterprise creed – could not possibly commend itself to a rational man; for it is possible to be both rational and exceedingly unpleasant.

Let me attempt to introduce at least some appearance of order into the rather large number of ragged ends that we now have before us. To be *irrational*, I take it, is to fail, or refuse, or be unable to recognize a *reason* – not, of course, in a case where it is genuinely disputable whether or not what is offered as a reason really is a reason, but where the offered reason is, in one way or another, a reason unquestionably. Being irrational, if so, is of course conceptually distinct, if not always in practice distinguishable, from being, say, unreasonable, or perverse, or foolish, or very thick in the head; for to be slow and clumsy in recognizing reasons, or eccentric or misguided in according proper weight to them when recognized, is different from refusing or being unable to recognize them at all. Now, if that is so, then it is of course not necessarily irrational to hold mistaken beliefs. For some mistaken beliefs there may be, or a particular person may have, very good reasons; and even where the balance of reasons may actually incline against some mistaken belief, the case may not be so clear as to convict of irrationality those who continue to hold it. Again, if that is so, it cannot be, I think, positively irrational to hold that certain reasons are outweighed by others; if, for instance, I grossly neglect my own interests for the sake of minor attendance upon the convenience of another person, you may think me foolish or unreasonable in taking that person's convenience as a reason outweighing essential attention to my own concerns, but my position would be genuinely *irrational*, I think, only if I did not see that there *was* any reason at all that could be urged against it.

Now, if that is so, we can see, I believe, why some philosophers have maintained that morality *must* have an irresistible claim upon rational acceptance – but also, I fear, why this is not really the case. What is true, I suggest, is that moral reasons really are reasons, and could not rationally be denied to be so. The argument for that would run, very summarily, as follows: a man who will suffer if he acts in a certain way has a reason for not so acting, there is reason for him not to do so. If, we may say, one points out to him that he will suffer if he so acts, he may indeed rationally reply 'Yes, but . . .' (and introduce some *other* reason), but he cannot rationally say 'I don't see that that has anything to do with it'. The latter response could evoke, I think, nothing but blank incomprehension. But if *his* consequential suffering is a reason for *him* not to act in a certain way, then consequential suffering is a reason against courses of action; for the suffering of other persons is not *different*, merely in not being his, from his; what makes my sufferings rationally relevant to practical questions is that they are sufferings, and not that they are mine. Thus, in so far as morality may be said, very crudely and elliptically indeed, to have for its object the mitigation of suffering, it could not, as I believe, be rationally denied that the considerations it adduces are at any rate genuinely *relevant* to questions of conduct, that what it offers as reasons in that regard are actually reasons. Well, that is indeed not nothing; but it does not really take us very far.

The reason why this does not take us far is simply that, in full-blooded 'acceptance' of morality, a great deal more than this is involved. While not denying that moral reasons are reasons, one may still deny that recognition of or allusion to them is ever *efficacious* – perhaps holding that, in general, the recognition of reasons is never an effective determinant of action, or perhaps merely that the recognition of these reasons is not. And whether or not that is so seems to be a question of fact, on which rational disagreement, I take it, is at least not impossible. Again, while not denying that moral reasons are reasons, and perhaps not denying either that recognition of them is sometimes efficacious, one may hold that, as reasons, they are not particularly compel-ling – that there may be other and stronger reasons by which they are outweighed. Perhaps it is more important that the arts should flourish than that moral wrong should be avoided; perhaps, while the sufferings of mankind are some sort of reason for and against courses of action, there is stronger reason not to accept that debilitating shackling of the strong and the adventurous which would be an inevitable condition of their alleviation, or that dis-abling violence to natural psychological impulses which moral virtue entails. In short: while a rational being, merely *qua* rational, may possibly be obliged to concede that what moral argument adduces as reasons really are reasons, I do not see that he can be obliged to concede – could not rationally deny – that morality really 'works', so to speak, as it is supposed to work, or that, in the balance with other reasons for and against doing things, moral reasons must be accorded very great or preponder-ant cogency. He may see what morality is, and think that there is not much in it. We are, unavoidably, involved here with issues as to what is true, and what is to be valued; and while not all opinions on these matters may be equally tenable, or reasonable, or uneccentric, these are issues on which rational beings may rationally differ. If so, then recognition of 'the moral law' as an *efficacious* and *predominant* determinant of practical judgement and action cannot be forced, so to speak, *a priori* upon rational beings.

·　　·　　·

How then, finally, do people come to 'recognize' morality at all?
If, as rational beings, they do not *have* to do so, how is it that they
do? The brief answer here has to be, I think, simply that it is
possible for them to come to *want to*. I do not mean by this that
it is possible completely to remove what I have been calling the
'limitation of human sympathies'. By the near prospect or the
reality of, say, suffering for oneself, or a parent, or a child, or a
friend, one will surely always be naturally *moved* as one is not by
the predicament of a total stranger, still less by the mere knowledge (which after all we all have all the time) that someone or
other is suffering somehow and somewhere. Morality does not in
that way expand, or at any rate does not expand without limit,
our human sympathies. But while one may be largely or completely *unmoved* by another's suffering, it is still possible to be not
indifferent to it, to want it *not to happen* – somewhat as, in one's own
case, it is possible to be not indifferent to some contingency, as it
might be one's financial situation in thirty years' time, notwithstanding that one is, here and now, not actually agitated, moved,
or affected by it; or as a judge in his court may want to do justice
between the claims of contending litigants, without personally
caring two hoots for either of them. But if one can be thus not
indifferent to the predicament of others – can want it to be, say,
better, notwithstanding that one is not actually agitated by its
being bad – then it is possible to come to want to comply with,
and want that others should comply with, principles whose recognition would tend to ameliorate that predicament. One can
want to acquire and exercise the settled disposition to comply
with such principles in one's judgement and conduct, to give
due weight to the range of reasons that those principles generate.
It may be that, if human beings could not ever actually be moved,
affected, stirred, by the predicament of *any* human being other
than themselves, then the amelioration of the human predicament
in general would be, and would remain, a matter of general indifference, something it would never occur to people, in any
way, to want; but if one can be (as most can be) moved *sometimes*
by the predicament of another, then it is possible for one to want
human predicaments to be in general ameliorated, and thus to
feel as practically efficacious that range of reasons which has that
ultimate *rationale*.

Thus, it is possible for a person to want to be moral; and a person is moral, by and large, exactly in proportion as he really wants to be so. We may thus say that, just as the *need* for morality, its having a point, derives from very general facts about human beings and their predicament, so also it is a fact about human beings that they are capable of morality; the disease and its remedy, so to speak, have a common source. But the essence of the remedy is not in reason; it is in non-indifference. Reason, in human affairs, is a plant of precarious, variable, always limited growth; so is non-indifference. And that is why the moral conscience, to adapt certain terms of Butler's, however great its 'authority', is of variable and limited 'power', and does not, as we see that it does not, 'govern the world'.

Index